The Encyclopedia of Red Flags

*A Guide to Peaceful Dating
for Women Who Are Looking
for "The One"
(And Don't Want to Get Screwed!)*

Jackie Blake

Wisdom Within Publishing

2013

For more information about her books, workshops and practice, visit Jackie Blake's blog at *www.soulmateinthecity.com*

•

TABLE OF CONTENTS

DEDICATION

This work is dedicated to my holistic healing coach and teacher John McMullin. I have no words to thank you for what you have done to help me grow as a woman and help others. You changed the direction of my life. Much of this book is derived from the work I did with you. I hope I did it justice. (More about John McMullin and his work can be found at *www.journeysofwisdom.com*).

This work is also dedicated to my best friend, Isabel De Los Rios, who had to listen to all of these stories for the past 14 years. You are my best friend, my unpaid therapist and a model of how I want to live my life. Ironically, you never would have needed this book because you somehow knew all of this already. Is every woman blessed with a best friend that can hold her in the highest regard, even when she doesn't hold herself there? If not, they should be. I only hope other women can find a friend like you who is an example of a woman who had the courage to follow the highest callings of her soul and is now in a happy marriage with good communication and can give her friends advice from a healed and whole place. I can't clone you, so the next best thing was to write this book.

FORWARD

Why You Need This Book. [Hint: Oxytocin]

You know the feeling. There is a very logical voice whispering in the back of your head. It's telling you to walk away. And you're trying pretty hard to listen to it, but it's being drowned out by a much more exciting, dramatic singing and dancing musical troupe, complete with brass band and tap-dancing shoes urging you, at full volume: "Jump in, jump in, jump in" ...

The operatic-singing-dancing-musical-chorus is oxytocin – the "love hormone" – that creates the "chemistry" we describe when we find ourselves warm and glowing after meeting someone we're physically attracted to. Even a small hug or kiss from this attractive individual can send absurd amounts of this powerful love-drug shooting through our bodies... each drop taking with it (and don't hold me to the science here) logical, rational thoughts.

Cue, *The Encyclopedia of Red Flags*.

As a coach, I saw it everyday in clients. As a single woman in her thirties, I have seen it plenty with my friends (and, of course, myself). Wonderfully sane individuals whose rose-tinted oxytocin glasses persuade them to romanticize situations that would normally make them run in the opposite direction. The tempestuous water looks inviting. You jump in. But suddenly you realize you've forgotten how to swim. Well, now Jackie's insightful book offers a lifejacket to grab onto when the love-drug tsunami arrives.

Why You Need Jackie. [Hint: Bawdy Spiritualism at its Best.]

I had worked as a business and life coach for a few years when I met Jackie. Despite having coaching tools up to my eyeballs, I couldn't get my fitness mojo on, so asked around for a recommendation for someone that matched my very specific, and totally contradictory, criteria for a personal trainer: someone who would push the hell out of me but be really easy on me, someone who'd make me burn but never make it hurt, and someone who'd kick me into action but never make me feel bad when I didn't perform.

Strut in Jackie Blake – a perfect blend of contradictions, with her small "I'll kick your butt" powerhouse body and her voluptuous "I'll seduce you before you know it" hair. With her can-do, straight-shooter attitude and her "don't mess with me" wiggle. All tied up with a huge smile and a warm, hearty laugh as she tells you like it is.

Jackie's natural kindness, spirituality and commitment to her work have an amazing way of making you feel totally comfortable and at ease while keeping you in-check – one of those unique women who somehow manage to squeeze deeply spiritual insights and outrageously bawdy jokes into the same sentence. A woman who has had her fair share of knocks, but just bounces right up with even better hair and a little more wiggle. So there's no one better to give you advice when the oxytocin kicks in and you need some serious sense knocked into you. Fast.

A Sanity Flashcard.

Here's the deal, ladies. It's not that you don't see the warning signs. You do. You know them well. You've been here before and so have your friends. So, you're going to read this book with an occasional flinch and a knowing nod of the head, "Yup, that was Tim… or Josh… or Joe." You can be sure you've met someone who'll fit the description. And you can be sure you'll groan as you recognize yourself too.

What I've learnt from my coaching clients and my friends is that knowing in and of itself doesn't always change behavior. We just dive in, time and again, with eyes wide shut.

The Encyclopedia of Red Flags helps you look beyond the "knowing" feeling to the "why." What's the pattern you're repeating? What does the situation trigger in you that makes it hard to let it go? How can you turn down the volume on the musical-troupe to have a sensible conversation about your future, about your safety and about your true worth? Jackie's book offers the insightful questions that move you from *knowing* to *acting differently*.

I made a flashcard with the gems of wisdom I picked up from Jackie's book. I'd like to pass these gems to clients, friends and random people in the street that looked like they may have succumbed to the brass band musical performance. I hope you will too.

- Listen with your instinct, not just your ears (or your oxytocin!)
- Save yourself ('cause you'll never save him)
- Have the courage to walk away (have faith in the big picture)
- Get curious about your own patterns and past, as well as (and before!) his

- Beware the conquer mentality (Alpha girls, you know who you are…)

A Caveat. [Be Open To Being Surprised.]

As you read this book, you'll feel like you're sitting with Jackie at home, curled up on your couch with a big mug of coffee, as she chats away to you about her dating experiences in New York. She'll make you laugh, she'll make you wince or cry, but she'll also center and empower you. You'll want to be her friend, and you'll feel like you are.

Because the book is just like Jackie: it'll push the hell out of you but be really easy on you, will make you burn but never make it hurt, and will kick you into action but never make you feel bad when you don't perform well.

Because, and here's the caveat, you'll still dive in. You'll still wear rose-tinted glasses. You'll still fall. And please, don't go losing that. Life is about taking risks, opening your heart and not letting someone else's garbage make you cynical about love. But, use Jackie's wonderful tips and guides to help ensure you don't lose yourself along the way.

And who knows, maybe someone will surprise you. Or even better, maybe you'll surprise yourself.

Nadia Tarazi

March 2013

DISCLAIMER

I use the word "God" throughout this book when describing my experience of a Higher Power. This word feels most natural to me. If that word does not resonate with your experience, please substitute it with Source, The Universe, Jesus, Love or any specific denomination or expression of God that works for you.

I am not a psychotherapist and this book is not meant to take the place of healing work with a qualified professional. I am a woman who has dated a lot of men in the search for love. I have made a lot of mistakes, have learned a tremendous amount through those mistakes and I learned to change myself and therefore change the men I attract. I have done a lot of therapy and taken seminars to learn to become a more mature and loving woman.

In this book, I am simply sharing what I've learned about dating with the hopes that it will help other women have a quicker learning curve to allow more love into their lives. I know that a lot of my readers cannot afford endless therapy sessions. This book offers clues into how you can get the ball rolling on healing your relationships and/or inability to attract a relationship.

INTRODUCTION

"When I am healed I am not healed alone."

– Lesson 137 of A Course in Miracles Workbook, pg. 261

I have dated everyone…

OK maybe not everyone, but when you really put yourself out there to meet men for so many years, it feels as if you have dated everyone. Some of these dates I have chronicled on my blog ~~*www.soulmateinthecity.com.*~~ *no longer in publication* So many of my fans kept writing to me saying, "You really should write a book. You've dated so much and done so much work on yourself. You've learned so much and your experiences could help so many people." I was reluctant at first but then one night I had the following dream:

I dreamed that I was at a consignment store. There were a bunch of dresses hanging on the racks. When I looked more closely at the dresses, I could see that they were made of human skins (almost like when Lady Gaga wore the dress made of meat to the MTV Video Music Awards). In the dream I heard a voice say, "now it's your turn" and I knew that it meant that it was time for me to take off my skin and sell it as a dress. According to *www.dreammoods.com* "to dream of your skin, represents protection or shield of your inner self. It serves as a physical boundary and how close you let others get to you." It was time for me to share my inner self and all that I had learned about relationships instead of hiding the wounds I'd sustained trying to figure it all out. I knew in the dream that the steps I've taken to heal those wounds could help so many people. I had the realization that Life is just one big consignment shop, where we sell (share) the experiences we've gained that we don't need to hang onto so tightly anymore to other people who will pay a lesser price to than we did to gain that experience through our eyes. I have certainly paid a lesser price to benefit from the knowledge of a great many authors and teachers and now it was my turn for others to benefit from me.

The other reason I decided to publish this book has to do with an episode of Oprah that really moved me. In this episode, Wynonna Judd was vulnerably sharing about the struggles she had gone through in life and her healing process. When Oprah asked her why she was sharing this with the world on the show, Judd said it was because a lot of her fans struggled with many of the same issues that she did, couldn't afford therapy and she wanted to help them by sharing the lessons from her own life. I really admired that. "That is a purposeful life," I thought. Now I do not pretend to have the same money available for therapy as Ms. Judd, but I have been blessed to receive the right therapy at crucial times in my life. For those who are seeking help with relationship patterns and not finding the help you need, I offer you my life lessons on a platter to learn from.

And so I wrote this book of red flags with regard to dating with one purpose in mind: to bring peace and understanding to the lives of women who are single and still looking for a life partner. I wrote it for women who may be frustrated with the process – feel like they always get it wrong, or are blaming men or stuck in self-blame. There is a more peaceful way to do this.

This book talks about many of the red flags that I have

encountered in my life while dating. What is a red flag? Basically it's something that a man says or does that raises a warning signal within you. A warning that he doesn't share your values, that he is not ready for a relationship or that he could be an emotionally or physically destructive person to get involved with. We often dismiss these early warnings because we so much want to connect with a man and are needy for attention and affection. Don't beat yourself up if you've done this because we've all done it to varying degrees. And you always look back to the moment when you could have nipped it in the bud…when he said or did that weird thing that made you think twice. Our intuition never lies. The way to learn from these experiences and hone your valuable intuitive abilities is to never make yourself wrong. Everyone is intuitive and especially women. We live in a culture that tells us to ignore our intuitive inclinations and instead just go to the doctor, take a pill, eat some comfort food, go shopping or drinking or any number of deflecting activities instead of dealing with the real issue we know we need to deal with. The more you listen to your intuition the more you will learn to trust it and the less you will make yourself wrong for the things that come up.

I've dated many, many men of different races, religions, ages and socio-economic groups for the past 15 years. And I've learned a lot. This book is a list of the collective red flags that have come up for me, and what I have learned from them.

What this book is NOT is a list of personality quirks that irritated me or other women. Personality quirks are not red flags. For example, if a guy insists on waking up at 4:47am everyday to get a jump on his workload and go to the gym before he gets to the office, this is not a sign that you are dealing with a potentially bad partner. This is a personality quirk of an extremely disciplined person. Either his habits work with your lifestyle, or they don't and that is for you alone to decide. But waking up early at the same random time everyday is not a universal red flag.

However, if said early riser also frequently refers to his ex-girlfriend as "Jennifer the Bitch," THAT is indeed a universal red flag. Speaking disrespectfully about one's ex-partner is always indicative that there are underlying issues that may crop up and sabotage your relationship.

A Little More About My Process...

Throughout my 20's and 30's, I was constantly involved in personal development groups, seminars and one-on-one therapy. When I decided to allow healing to come to me, it always did. It just blew my mind that when I healed a particular issue within myself, the type of man that I attracted after that healing also changed. My relationships became more fulfilling and loving and each partner I attracted was "better" than the last. (Really, he just met me at the new level of openness and self love that I had attained. When you are stuck in an issue within yourself, you actually can't see the great available guys that are all around you).

There are no accidents in life. If you are being presented with a certain side of a man's personality, there's a reason. You can choose to sweep it under the rug, or you can look at it dead in the eye for the deeper truths that it may reveal. If you consistently attract a certain type of man in a way that is distressing to you, there is most certainly an unhealed pattern within yourself that Life keeps giving you opportunities to heal. And you will continue to attract that pattern until you get it "right." (Right = responding from love, most importantly love for oneself). I often attracted the same "dysfunctional" pattern in different men in succession until I learned how to deal with it in a loving way. (Hint: loving does not always mean sticking around; sometimes the loving thing to do is walk out the door; allowing disrespect or abuse to continue, is not loving).

Mirrors

Indeed many of the men we date are mirrors. A mirror is someone who reflects back to you something about yourself. When you either really love or really hate something about another person, those are YOUR qualities that you are loving or hating. You would not have such a strong emotional charge on those qualities if they were not your own. For example, if you hate that a man you are dating is emotionally checked-out, ask yourself if you are emotionally checked out. It can be extremely embarrassing or even painful to look into a mirror of your own negative qualities through another person who is exhibiting them, but it is IMPORTANT for self-growth. A man's red flags may very well mirror your own. Sometimes a man may mirror qualities that we had in the past that we have healed. Then the lesson may be to observe how it feels to be treated that way and acknowledge whom we may have treated that way in the past and make amends if necessary. To make amends means to put it right. Either apologize to that person in person or if that's not possible or appropriate then privately acknowledge that you are sorry for how you behaved and vow to do better in the future. Also, forgive yourself for your behavior.

If you are angry that the man you are dating is not giving to the relationship, ask yourself if you are giving, or if you are over-giving! According to A Course in Miracles, "Only what you have not given can be lacking in any situation." Sometimes the growth is to learn to initiate giving love and affection, and sometimes it's to learn to give a person space and/or time.

Angels

Some of the men we date are angels. "A Human Angel is a person who makes a commitment to be placed by spirit at exactly the right juncture of time and space to make a positive contribution in the life of another human." *(http://www.humanangel.com)*. We've all met people like this; people who have changed the direction of our lives with positive feedback, helpful suggestions, leading the way by example, a smile, a gift or just simply loving us exactly as we are. Many of you have been a human angel to someone. What can be painful about dating an angel is that we often project our newfound happiness and salvation onto him when really he simply opened a door for us to experience ourselves as happy and loved, as bigger and more emotionally expansive than we were before. We want him to stay forever. And, while it's possible that we may be his "lifetime assignment" and end up getting married, perhaps he was only meant to come into our life for a short time and/or a specific reason. If he does leave and he was an angel, you will know exactly what gift he brought you and hopefully you will be able to accept it with gratitude and allow him to go to be where he needs to be next.

Sometimes angels bring what we would call a negative

experience to our lives. It's hard to see, but this is a gift as well. Challenging experiences often teach us self-reliance and inner strength. They test our faith and teach us the power of surrender. They can show us where we were blocking love from coming into our lives.

How Soon Will Red Flags Start to Arise?

There is no "too soon" for red flags. Sometimes they come up in the first conversation, the first email or the first text message. Don't ignore them. I've said for years that you know everything you need to know about a man in 3 dates if you really *LISTEN* and *OBSERVE*. If you have been aware during your dates, there should be no real surprises later on unless you are dealing with a true sociopath. According to *www.dictionary.com*, a sociopath is "a person with a psychopathic personality whose behavior is antisocial, often criminal, and who lacks a sense of moral responsibility or social conscience." Sociopaths are unbelievably charming. They have no problem lying and are quite good at it. (Many can even pass a lie detector test so don't feel bad if you fall for it). They don't feel guilt, shame or remorse for lying and roping people in to their scams. It may take a little longer than 3 dates to realize you are dealing with a sociopath but you will certainly be able to see his true colors in 3 months of dating which is why it's important to keep your eyes open at the beginning as he's making you fall in love with him. Enjoy the courtship but don't get overly addicted or attached to the seduction. Yes, you are amazing but a sociopath is able to convince most any woman that he loves her and that's she's amazing. In any case, if he is a sociopath his deception will unfold as the months pass as long as your eyes are open and you are not putting your head in the sand.

If you are reading this book, it's likely that like me, you grew up in the *Oprah Winfrey Show* era, where people put their problems on national television for all to see. Oprah has done countless shows on women whose husbands were living a double life and claimed they had no idea. And while they may have had no idea about the extent of the double life (their husbands were running Ponzi schemes, selling body parts on the black market, selling drugs or other illegal or immoral activities) there were always signs that something was amiss: affairs, secrecy, little lies, disappearances, strange credit card charges, etc. These women didn't ask questions until the crap finally hit the fan and there were police swarming their home at 5am. In retrospect, all of these women knew that something was wrong and were afraid to uncover the truth because they knew it would shake the entire foundation of what they thought their life was built upon. Sometimes it feels safer not to see things. Some didn't ask questions because they were kept up in nice lifestyles by these men and didn't want to rock the boat. Watching these programs shows us the ramifications of brushing red flags under the rug and hoping they will go away. The truth comes out sooner or later and when it's later the consequences are usually much worse. Keeping quiet and pretending to be the innocent woman will not work. In one way or another, we all have to step up and take responsibility for what we are involved in.

Normal men have remorse and guilt about lying to and manipulating women so it will be easier to know their intentions sooner. But even still the flood of hormones that rush a man's body when he is attracted to you will drive him to say or do almost anything to sleep with you so give it some time to make sure these claims and actions are legitimate. (Not to mention the flood of hormones rushing through your body make you more apt to believe him.)

The red flags I have listed in this book are things that can clue you into what kind of man you are dealing with early on. Truthfully, you can probably tell everything you need to know about a man in 15 minutes but give it 3 dates if you feel you need to be sure before you rule someone out as potential.

Soulmates

I've heard many spiritual experts say the magnetic attraction you feel when you meet someone means you are meeting a soulmate. It doesn't mean that things will always be easy with this person, but you can surely tell when you have met a soulmate, even in 5 minutes. This is what people call love at first sight. It's not love really, it's "this person is super attractive to me which means there's a powerful lesson for me in getting involved with them" at first sight. As Marianne Williamson says, "God brings together the two people who have the maximal potential for growth from being romantically involved with each other" (Williamson 33). So sometimes, when things get hard, it's not time to run but time to stick in and see where there can be growth.

Many ask, what is a soulmate? Here's my best definition, as I understand it. A soulmate is someone we recognize on the level of the soul. We "knew" them before we incarnated, that is why often they seem so familiar even if you have only just met. You and your soulmate made an agreement before your incarnation that you would create certain experiences for each other so that you could both come to know yourselves more deeply. Lovers, family and friends can all be soulmates. You cannot "miss" a soulmate. If you were intended to meet in this lifetime, you will. You can delay the meeting or dismiss them when you meet them, but if they are indeed your soulmate, they will continue to come into your life until the highest purpose of the relationship is served. As it says in *A Course in Miracles*, "All who meet will someday meet again until their relationship becomes holy" (ACIM 67). In this context, "holy" means loving, peaceful, forgiving and compassionate. Even if a man has wronged you badly, can you forgive him, release him and understand the wounds in him that brought about his behavior and move on with peace in your heart? Pay close attention to who comes into your life and to whom you are attracted. What is the lesson to be learned from this person? You can either face it head-on now or continue to drag along the same issues with the same person (or others just like him) for many years (and lifetimes) to come.

Twin Souls

A twin soul is considered one's ultimate soulmate, the one and only other half of one's soul. There is a Greek myth that talks about how humans originally were joint beings with two heads, four arms and four legs. We were already attached to our twin soul. But Zeus, fearing our power, split the humans in half condemning them to spend the rest of their lives trying to find the other half of their soul to finally be complete.

Now I don't actually believe that this is true exactly as it is written in this myth. I've heard it described another way in *Twin Souls: Finding Your True Spiritual Partner*.

The twin soul is the partner that completes you, however the only way to find them is to become complete in and of yourself. When you stay on the path of bringing yourself into wholeness, the twin soul will present him or herself (Joudry and Pressman 21).

So, what does it mean to become complete, in and of yourself? Well of course it's different for everyone but I think what we could all stand to examine in the name of completeness is learning to balance and hone both our masculine and feminine energies. Masculine energy is aggressive, initiating, logical, doing. Feminine energy is passive, receptive, intuitive, being. Specifically for us as women, when our masculine energy is overly dominant, it is hard for a man to stay around us for very long because if he does he will have to take the feminine role. Either that or the only men that will stay around us will have overly dominant feminine energy. For example, if you are a predominantly masculine-energy woman (like me), can you learn to be still, quiet, receptive, feeling, vulnerable and sensual? These qualities would bring you more into balance and completeness and allow you to receive a masculine man.

expanded upon

As Joudry and Pressman put it:

> It could almost be said that the twin appears on the scene when least needed, when each half-soul has reached its highest point of independence in the divided state. This is also the pinnacle of aloneness. Every man and every woman must climb the mountain alone, able to stand firm against the high winds that buffet the elevated soul. It is then, out of the mist, that the twin appears, not in response to

emotional need but to fulfill the deepest need of the soul. By the marvelous design of the Divine Planner, the ultimate loneliness of the spirit gives way to the first great joining and the end of loneliness forever. (Joudry and Pressman 21)

Twin souls recognize each other with absolute certainty. If a man has left you for someone else, he was not your twin soul because twin souls are unable to abandon each other (Joudry and Pressman 10). In other words, if someone is really for you, you can't lose him.

The one thing that always denotes a twin soul relationship is that the world is better for your having come together. It's not that you meet your twin soul and then hole yourself up on a paradise island for the rest of your lives so that everything can be perfect. It's more that you both become your best selves in each other's presence and have more to give to the world (Joudry and Pressman 19-20). Here's a hint: if you meet a man that you think is your twin soul, except he has a wife and 3 kids and he abandons them to run off with you, this is not your twin soul. Evolved souls do not run out on those whom they've caused to become dependent on them. This is infatuation and will ultimately come crashing down because it is not sustainable. If he does end a relationship to be with you, it is done with honesty and integrity and he will provide financially and emotionally for any dependents.

Stages of a Relationship and Red Flags

Dr. Patricia Allen calls the first 3 months of any relationship "The Perfect Phase." During this time "you feel as though you have finally met the one person on earth who is 'right' for you. This is the time when the rosy glow of romance colors everything. Everything the two of you do and say is perfect" (Allen 111). We've all been through this wonderful period of relationships also known as infatuation. Both people are putting their best foot forward and minding their p's and q's. Of course, it's possible in "The Perfect Phase" to spot red flags, but we often ignore them or sweep them under the rug.

If you really are attracted to a man, there is absolutely nothing wrong with continuing with him while noting a red flag, if he is of high character and striving to be the best man he can be. No man you meet will be perfect and Dr. Allen suggests that if he is at least "51%" good to see the relationship through to completion (Allen 167).

The next 3 months of a relationship, months 3-6, are called "The Imperfect Phase." "At this point, people usually feel comfortable enough with each other to get off their best behavior and, in effect, 'be themselves.'" -- Hello red flags! -- "This is when you learn what you already knew but didn't want to admit, that nobody is perfect, including your newfound love" (Allen 163). During this phase, you sober up a bit and see the shadow side of the man you are dating. You may see him get jealous of your male friends where before he was totally secure. He may start to admit parts of his past that involve promiscuous sexuality or raging anger that he didn't tell you before. You may see him flip out on a waiter, a cab driver or you, whereas before he was gentle and kind. Only you can ascertain which behaviors are deal-breakers and which are acceptable. But remember, no man is perfect. If he is mostly good, keep him (Allen 167).

Changing Your Pattern of Attraction

*"It takes courage...to endure the sharp pains of self discovery
rather than choose to take the dull pain of unconsciousness that
would last the rest of our lives."*
                    – Marianne Williamson, *A Return to Love*

This is not a book to encourage pointing fingers or
bitching about men. It is a book to encourage growth.
There are many books on dating and how men should
behave, ad nauseum. But what happens if you are not
attracting men that treat you with courtesy and caring?
Are you just supposed to be alone? Well, yes, perhaps
for a just little while until you change your attraction
pattern in the area of romantic relationships. Since the
definition of insanity is doing the same thing over and
over and expecting different results, it's time to change
your thought patterns, the questions you ask yourself
and consequently your words and behaviors.

I believe that we attract what we are, what we expect
and what we believe we deserve. After each red flag, I
have provided a few mental thought patterns and
beliefs that you may hold that could be causing you to
attract a man with a particular red flag. Ask yourself
the questions I've provided and see if they are true for
you. If they are, it's time to examine where that belief
came from and choose a new belief. And while
backtracking to where the belief initially came from can
be a fascinating and liberating exploration into oneself,
the most important part of this exercise by far is to
choose the new belief that you would like to foster in
your life. For example, knowing that you choose
emotionally unavailable men because your father was
emotionally unavailable and that is what feels like love
to you is great for understanding your patterns. But

until you believe, "I deserve to be loved demonstratively and I accept it now" or "I am totally worthy of love" you will not attract a new type of man.

"Relationships are assignments" (Williamson 107). What does this mean? I think it means that God is constantly bringing people into our lives that have something to teach or show us about ourselves by being in relationship with them. We are assigned to different people to bring about healing in them and us. Sometimes these assignments will last a few months and sometimes they will last for the rest of your life. How do we know when a person we meet is our intended assignment (also known as our soulmate)? We absolutely feel magnetized to them and don't fully understand why. They look beautiful and attractive to us. We feel a connection. Whenever this happens, you know you have met your next assignment. *to run- This is usually when one of us wants like they date*

Now what if your assignment has one of the red flags listed below, which is very likely. Your assignment will not be easy or perfect. So, if he is flawed, is it time to *with me,* run? Maybe or maybe not, only you can decide that. *I felt* This book is intended to be more of an informational *chosen she* tool to give you insight into what is going on with him *he felt* or yourself if you bump up against a red flag so that *out of shape* you can proceed with caution, protect yourself *we liked each* emotionally and physically and bring more *other but had to* understanding. Is it possible that this man attracted you *deal* into his life because he wants to change, grow and learn *with any* to love and you may be the angel that gives him the *own* chance to do so? Absolutely. Or perhaps he's not ready *with the* yet, another very real possibility. It's really a case-by- *insecurities* case basis for you to investigate. *If his masculine energy did* If you decide a man is not for you, that's fine. But to really *magnetism scare you - using it as an opportunity to learn to trust.*

15

glean the lessons from the interaction and move on with peace and openness, take inventory of the qualities you liked about him and those that you didn't. You get what you focus on so while you want to certainly acknowledge and note the qualities you didn't like, you don't want to dwell on them for too long because then those negative qualities will stay in your vibrational field and will show up somewhere else in your life. Constantly bitching and rehashing the negative aspects of what happened while taking no ownership of your own role in those events, is only going to hurt you, not him.

Where we fail to complete in one area, we will certainly recreate in another. What that means is, if you must end a relationship do so with honesty, compassion and the intention to leave peace behind you. For if you don't the problems in the current relationship will follow you into your next partnership. When you run away, you bring yourself with you. If you have chosen not to be with a man because of his shortcomings, your involvement with him or others like him will only be complete if you forgive his behavior. Remember, to forgive does not mean that you are making his behavior acceptable. It just means that you are willing to let go of the anger and move on with your life. Ask yourself where he must be coming from within himself to exhibit those behaviors. What must have happened in his life to cause these behaviors to manifest? If you mentally or verbally harp on what a jackass he is, you will certainly attract more jackass behavior from him and more jackasses in other parts of your life. The outer world is a reflection of what's going on in your inner world. Forgive, learn, move on and find a way to focus on the qualities that you loved in him while accepting that as a whole he is not for you. If you can't forgive, then pray to be able to forgive. Give your feelings about this man over to God so that He can bring you out of fear and into love.

Taking Things Personally

On the one hand, you don't want to take his behavior too personally. In fact, this is the second agreement in the powerful book *The Four Agreements: A Practical Guide to Personal Freedom* by Don Miguel Ruiz. The way people behave is more often about them than you. When we take things personally, we accept the emotional poison that someone else is offering. We do this because we want to believe that we are so powerful as to cause another human to become sad or angry or behave in crazy ways. But this is not true. As Ruiz says, "Nothing other people do is because of you. It is because of themselves. All people live in their own dream, in their own mind; they are in a completely different world from the one we live in. When we take something personally, we make the assumption that they know what is in our world, and we try to impose our world on their world" (Ruiz 48).

For example, I was once newly dating a guy. We had gone on about four dates and he wanted to have sex with me. I didn't feel like I knew him well enough and I wasn't comfortable with being intimate with him at that point so I didn't have sex with him. He pretty much flipped out and told me that he was angry that I was holding out on him. He accused me of not treating him well and being mean to him. In my mind I was trying to create an atmosphere of emotional intimacy between us before rushing into physical intimacy, but in his mind I was purposely torturing him to try to control the relationship and get him to spend as much money on me as possible. Nothing could have been further from the truth but he was viewing me through the lens of what other women had done to him in the past. No matter how much I tried to explain to him where I was coming from, he insisted on holding me in the role of the "evil woman" in his life. I'll admit, for a moment, I did take it very personally and I wondered what I did to make him so angry. But then I realized that he had this relationship with all women in his life (beginning with his mother who was physically and emotionally abusive to him, even into his teen years). It had nothing to do with me.

On the other hand, you want to honestly look at the ways in which you may have contributed to his acting out, accepted the emotional poison and/or made it easy for him to take advantage of you. Good questions to ask are, "What was missing from my behavior?" "Where did I act out of fear?" and "Where did I fail to recognize the signs?" In the example discussed above, my own insecurity about my worth as a woman caused me to accept this man's accusations that I was cold and neglectful. It had been a long time since I was in a happy relationship and his words were mirroring back to me things that part of me believed about myself. These dramas can play out in many different ways but we change the pattern of attraction when we acknowledge our role in its creation, even if it was a very small role. You only have control over cleaning up your side of the bed.

Here are the assumptions that I'm operating under:

First and foremost, that you are looking for love and that some part of you knows that the surest path is by loving yourself and growing into a mature woman.

That's who this book is for. Nowadays with I
dating, it's remarkably easy to fill one's sche
dates and sex from an endless merry-go-rou
taking absolutely no personal stock of the p
are showing up in one's life. And while this may be an
appropriate exploration for young women in their 20's,
I don't recommend it for too long, and certainly not in
your 30's and beyond. It's tedious and repetitive.
Drama-filled yet incredibly boring because you never
actually get anywhere. And there is another way.

A great way to really get to know the man you are
dealing with is to not have sex with him until he has
committed to you and has made it clear that he wants
to be in a relationship with you. I know it sounds
archaic, but it works. Doing this will insure that you
never have that awkward time of feeling like you are
giving everything and wondering when or what you
are going to get back. That time is wrought with red
flags and they are all usually too late because you're
hooked. If the sex is good and you've already fallen for
this guy it's hard to break free.

According to *Getting to "I DO"*, "A man knows before
he meets a woman if he is available for commitment,
but often what it takes is a woman requiring him to
make that commitment" (Allen 122). This means three
things:

1) Let him take the lead in the relationship and ask
   you out on dates. If he's not trying to take you
   on dates he is not serious. If he doesn't ask you
   out or just tries to get you to go back to his
   apartment, move on. (The "let's watch a movie
   at my apartment" suggestion for a second date
   probably means he's only interested in one

thing). These are red flags and they just saved you from a whole lot of crap.

2) Ask a man within the first few dates what he is looking for. Most likely, he will tell the truth about whether he's looking for a relationship or just some fun. And even if he says that he's just looking to have fun, this doesn't necessarily mean that you should run away. It does mean that you should keep your expectations in check, not put all of your hopes into him and definitely keep dating other people. (Although of course men know what we want to hear so some of them flat out lie. This is why you must do #3.)

3) Make him wait for sex for at least 1-2 months of consistent dating to make sure he is telling the truth and that you actually know whom you are sleeping with. (Actually both relationship authors Dr. Pat Allen AND Steve Harvey recommend waiting 3 months to sleep with someone but I must tell you in my experience and in the experience of every single one of my non-religious friends, this is an excessive amount of time.) Very few men will continue dating you for 2 months without sex if they are not serious about you so probably the ones that are sticking around are pretty serious. The men who are just playing games or trying to use you for sex will realize that you are not available for an easy roll in the hay. They'll simply move on to someone who's a little easier. And if that's the case, then good riddance!

(In my experience a man that sticks around for longer than 3 months without sex is suspect. What is he doing to get his sexual needs met outside of what's going on between the two of you? Heck, what are you doing to get your sexual needs met outside of him? I mean we're all grown adults here with natural and normal physical needs.)

Yes, I know it sucks that you have to wait so long, but trust me you do. A woman who gives up sex too quickly is not a slut. But in a man's eyes, she is playing a man's game and showing that her emotional standards are very low. As far as he's concerned it's "every man for himself, even if one of them is a woman." (Allen 124) And it's the same with cherishing your feelings. If you have not made yourself vulnerable and honest by stating that you only want to have sex within the bounds of a committed relationship, then you may be just a playmate to him, like one of the guys except with a vagina. And that does not feel good ladies and you know it.

If this is hard for you, ask yourself why you are afraid to share your true feelings about wanting a relationship with a man. Do you feel that there are no good men left so you should just take what you can get even if it's substandard treatment? You know that's not true. Every woman deserves to be treated well and there are plenty of good men out there. Are you afraid to admit to yourself that you want a relationship because it's been so hard to find one? Are you afraid that he's not going to want the same thing and that will imply that you are not good enough? You also know that's not true. A man decides what he wants for himself regardless of who you are. It's true that sometimes a specific woman's qualities will wake a man up to the things he's been missing in his life, but your worth is not based on whether or not he sees those qualities in you because that is outside of your control. Yes, it may sting if a man that you really like doesn't feel the same way about you. Sometimes it's downright baffling. But he is NOT the last man on earth and you will recover and move on to date other great guys.

Another note about the sex thing:

OK ladies. Let's just get real. All this waiting around for sex can be really frustrating. I know, I've been there. For years, I had a scant amount of sex because I was looking to have sex only within the bounds of a committed relationship. And the relationship that I wanted just wasn't happening. Now granted I didn't get "taken for a ride" by some ill-intentioned guy, but I ate more chocolate than any 5'1" woman should eat, EVER! We always find some outlet for an unmet need. We are sexual beings and expressing ourselves sexually is a natural and normal part of life. (Not to mention a fun and beautiful part as well.) While reckless, wanton sexuality certainly does not serve to bring us a committed relationship, abstinence also may not serve to bring us peace in the process of bringing in a relationship. Unless you believe it does. This is a very personal thing. I'm simply offering an option for women who want to continue to express their sexuality while attracting a committed relationship. Some women need a time of less sexual activity, perhaps after the wildness that has become our 20's, to reclaim and redefine what they want out of a sexual relationship. Explore what feels best to you, but if you do not want to shut down your sexuality on the quest for committed love then here is my advice:

1) Become familiar with the art of self-pleasure. In a perfect world, we would all have a loving

sexual relationship and be able to fulfill these needs with a partner whenever we want. If this is not the case, it is extremely helpful to be able to take care of the urge when it arises. This will also help you determine what you like sexually and how you like to be touched so that when you do have a partner you will be better able to communicate your desires.

2) While you are looking for love, I recommend taking a "lover." What is a lover? Well according to the Free Online Merriam-Webster Dictionary, it's:

   A) A person in love, especially a man in love with a woman

   B) An affectionate or benevolent friend

   C) A person with whom one has sexual relations.

These three elements are the holy grail of the lover. The only major difference between a lover and a partner is that with a lover there is no attachment or concern about whether you will fit into each other's lives in the long run. It is agreed upon that you are entering into a mutually respectful and enjoyable sexual (and perhaps romantic) relationship based on being present in the moment. Be careful when taking a male friend or co-worker as a lover because this can quickly become confusing.

Taking a "lover" is different than taking a "booty call." A booty call is generally someone you don't like talking to in the light of day. Whether you like it or not, when you have sex with someone you share energy with him. That's right, you take on some of his energy and he takes on some of yours. Some metaphysical practitioners believe that we have a lifelong energetic bond to every person we've had sexual intercourse with. So, it's really a good idea to make sure that you only engage sexually with people that you would at least like to have a conversation with as a bare minimum requirement.

A synonym to "lover" is a "paramour" which is "a person with whom someone is having a romantic or sexual relationship and especially a secret or improper relationship." Lovers are best kept secret (for the most part, with the exception of a trusted friend) and are generally even more delicious when they are improper. And by improper I do not mean married or otherwise taken. It can mean older, younger, of a different religion, from a different country, a man you could never bring home to meet your parents, a starving artist, traveling musician, someone in an "open" relationship, etc. I've found that it can really take the pressure off a sexual relationship to know that the two of you could never be together in the real world. Something about it can help you to just enjoy what you have in the moment. And still you never know, your paramour could become your partner. It happens. But most importantly, be truthful with yourself and honor your own needs. At the very least a relationship with a lover/paramour must consist of:

1) Good sex, sex that is enjoyable to BOTH partners. If the sex is not fulfilling, this sort of entanglement will serve to bring you down instead of up.

2) R-E-S-P-E-C-T. How do you know if you're being respected? For me it feels like a man and I

just shared an experience as opposed to feeling like he took the experience without giving anything in return.

There are two potential downsides to taking a "lover." First is that it's easy to become "the lazy dater." Your sexual needs are met by your lover and maybe in part some of your emotional needs and your need for excitement. This is when some women make the mistake of becoming complacent and not continuing to reach for what they really want in a relationship from a partner who can give it to them. If your lover does not want a relationship, you still have to keep putting yourself out into the world to meet other men who are available for the kind of relationship you want. For me one of the major positive aspects to sexual abstinence outside of a committed relationship is that it makes you hungry to get out into the world and meet available guys. There's nothing like not having sex to put a real fire under your behind and make you go to parties and sign up for Internet dating.

The other potential downside is that feelings can get involved before you know it. At some point when you are having good sex with someone there is pretty much guaranteed to be moments of vulnerability. I don't think it's possible to have good sex without moments of vulnerability because good sex implies communication between partners. Communicating what one likes sexually is a deeply vulnerable act. We women tend to develop feelings for a guy when we are vulnerable with him and especially when he is vulnerable with us. My advice for this is to take an honest appraisal of where you are with regard to your lover and end it if it is causing you more pain than joy. And just like in a relationship, a male lover should be the primary initiator of rendezvous. Men like to hunt and work for things. It's amazing to me how whenever I start initiating times to meet with a lover he always starts to lose interest. When I let a lover come after me, he keeps coming because he likes the conquest.

So consider carefully when taking a lover, but just know that as a fully-grown adult no one has the right to shame you for wanting to express yourself sexually.

Where to begin the process of attracting a relationship?

Begin with "the list." The list is all of the qualities that your perfect partner would have if you could craft the perfect man. At the top of the page write, "my romantic partner is" and then begin your list. It can include: kind, intelligent, sexy, ambitious, smart with money, compassionate, sensual, enjoys exercise, or anything else that is important to you. Don't hold back. Write everything you desire in a partner.

Obviously, you can put physical characteristics as well but I like to leave these as open as possible because you don't know what package God is going to put your partner in. He could be of an ethnicity you never considered dating. He could be "too short." He could be a little chunkier or skinnier than you'd been looking for. But ladies, I ask you to keep an open mind when it comes to the man who is going to love you for the rest of your life. God may line up the most perfect man for you and you will miss him because you were looking for someone else. Don't let it happen. The man who will ultimately steal your heart and be there for you through hell and high water may not look like what you thought he would look like. Look with your heart.

Remember the phrase "be careful what you wish for because you may just get it." Sometimes "the list" exercise brings up parts of ourselves that are not healed so we attract them in a partner. When I first did the list, I joked that the next man that I attracted would have parents who were deceased so I wouldn't have to deal with any more crap. (I was having a particularly challenging time with my own parents and was just venting- albeit viciously). Well wouldn't you know the next guy I met online did have deceased parents and a lot of remaining anger about it! He was a complete mess. The men you attract often are mirrors showing you the places that you still need to heal. This brought attention to the fact that I truly needed to heal my relationship with my parents. And when I did, I met more loving types of men, who did not have this problem.

Once you have made the list say, "Thank you for this man or someone better" to the Universe. And then keep your eyes open for what the Universe brings your way. It may be what you have written to a T if that is what would best serve you at this time. And it may not. I love the saying, "if you want to make God laugh, make plans." Let God know your intentions, but know in your heart that He will send you what is best for you anyway. "Be grateful for whoever comes, because each has been sent as a guide from beyond." -Rumi

Neale Donald Walsch puts this in a way I really like. He says:

> With regard to relationships or anything else in life, I like to get very specific about what it is that I would choose. And after I've allowed myself to be very, very specific, I take what

shows up. And the reason that I do that is that I never stop God from performing the miracles that She devises. And I never try to tell God what something should specifically look like, but merely what my idea about it is, in the moment." (Walsch 65)

Can we begin to do this? Can we tell God what we think we want and then keep our eyes open for what comes, knowing that a blessing and a lesson, either temporary or lifelong, resides in this person? I think this is the best strategy with regard to relationships (or really anything for that matter).

And don't worry that by becoming more spiritually aware and creating intentions that the fun and drama will leave your romantic life. As Marianne Williamson says in her audiobook *Romantic Relationships*, only the "cheap drama" will go away: like your boyfriend getting someone else pregnant – cheap drama; as opposed to you and your boyfriend learning to communicate from the heart – high drama. Having a man you already knew was unavailable, "abandon" you – cheap drama; having your partner's support while you are going through a tragedy – high drama. Cheap drama: receiving a barrage of stalking text messages from the same person; high drama: receiving a barrage of attention from his boisterous family, during the holidays. You get the point.

THE RED FLAGS

Note: some rude or strange behavior is not a red flag but actually mental illness.

For example, an autistic man has trouble reading social cues and emotions and may seem to be rude or afraid of intimacy, when really he is just trying his best within the constraints of his handicap.

A man who is serious about you should divulge his mental health history so that you can be compassionate and understanding.

I would still consult a mental health professional so that you can learn about how to communicate best with a man with mental illness, if you are so inclined to continue with him. But in the absence of *DIAGNOSED* mental illness, the following red flags apply.

NEWLY DATING RED FLAGS

"When you meet anyone, remember it is a holy encounter. As you see him, you will see yourself. As you treat him, you will treat yourself. As you think of him, you will think of yourself. Never forget this, for in him you will find yourself or lose yourself."

—A Course in Miracles

"When someone shows you who they are, believe them the first time."

—Maya Angelou

He speaks badly about his mother.

I don't care if she was a monster and did horrific things. No matter what she did to him, a man who has not made peace with his mother will ultimately turn on you. Without realizing it, you may be sucked in to reenacting his childhood dramas with him. He will find a way to accuse you of being the same way his mother was whether it was meddling, neglectful, abusive, bitchy, maniacal, etc. His judgments of his mother are in *HIS* energy field and are part of *HIS* Law of

Attraction. You will have no choice but to fulfill those judgments to agree with his experience of women in general. (A man's relationship with his mother or female caretaker is the blueprint for what he will create with women for the rest of his life). I repeat, how he judges her, is how he will judge you. He will actually teach you how to abuse him if he has not healed his relationship with her. For this reason it is extremely important to ask a man you are dating, "what was your experience of your mother?" or even a simple, "so tell me about your family." And then be still and listen to his answer.

Again, it is one thing for a man to objectively describe the events of his past, and then subjectively talk about how he experienced them. It is another thing entirely to bash one's flesh and blood. As my own personal therapist, John McMullin, has told me, "a man needs to respect his mother. He does not need to respect her behaviors, but needs to respect that she gave him life and brought him into the world and acknowledge that what he chooses to do with the life he was given is up to him. What he chooses to do with his relationship with her is up to him as well."

*This happened to me. I once met a man on *eHarmony.com* and in the open-ended question portion of the website's guided communication process, he asked me to "describe your early childhood experiences with your parents." (Personally, I think the fact that he asked this to a complete stranger is red flag as to his lack of discretion.) Being new to the site, I answered the question as honestly as possible and then turned it back on him. He began with: "My mother, if you can even call her that..." and began to describe in detail how mean she was to him. I should have blocked him and had absolutely no more to do with him. Even if his mother was truly horrible, he was disrespecting himself by disrespecting her. I met with the guy and let's just say the number of red flags he exhibited in that first meeting was way too many to count so I just ended the date quickly. But I could've easily avoided the waste of time. A man who speaks disrespectfully about his mother is an absolute red flag. He has obviously not even begun the process of reconciling his past. Run in other direction immediately.

The key here is that if he hasn't begun the work on healing his relationship with his mother, he will not be entirely available right now. He is not broken forever. No one is broken beyond repair. But ask yourself, "Is this man inviting healing into his life from what I can see?" Also, know that you can't begin, rush or force his process. A) It doesn't work. Every adult grows at his own pace, and B) If you do he will see you as trying to gain hierarchical power over him (like a mother or teacher would have). Men don't like to feel inferior to their women and they will quickly find their way out of the relationship. Whereas, if you acknowledge that a man you like may have "mommy-issues" and you remain a friend to him while he goes through the process of healing, one day, *if he is meant to be for you*, he will come back to you as a mature man ready to be available to you.

Why you may have attracted this:

- Have you made peace with and forgiven your own mother (or father)? Like attracts like and if not, this man may be a mirror into what's going on with you. If this is something you are struggling with, have you considered what your mother's childhood/upbringing was like to have created those behaviors in her?

- Do you have the need to be a rescuer? A rescuer will surely attract a victim/child, not a mature man.

- Do you believe that you or women in general are bad or evil (Eve eating the apple religious dogma-type stuff) and don't deserve to be treated well or spoken about with respect?

He speaks badly about his father.

Once again, even if his father was the most horrible person that did awful things, a man who has a strong negative charge on his father may end up carrying out exactly the behaviors that he finds so abhorrent. Why? Because we get what we focus on, and if he's focused on his father's alcoholic, abusive, or neglectful behavior, he is doomed to repeat it. Once again, to disrespect one's father is to disrespect oneself because that is disrespecting how we got on the planet in the first place. He may choose to disagree with his father's actions, but must respect his father as the man that gave him life if he is to become a whole man.

A man who can speak honestly about the parts of his father's behavior that he does and does not want to recreate is giving you an important window into his soul and is a man on the road to healing. Once again, it is important to ask a man about his experience of his father or significant paternal role model(s).

One particularly sad manifestation of this is a man who

still harbors a lot of anger because his father either abandoned the family or didn't even care to know him in the first place. If this man hasn't found the self-esteem to validate his own existence, NOTHING you do will validate it for him. Tread carefully until you assess where he is on his personal journey of validation as a man.

*This happened to me. Sometimes it's not even what he says but HOW he says it. I once met a man on *Match.com*. I was on the rebound from a particularly painful breakup and this guy was absolutely gorgeous so I went out with him. On our 2nd date, I asked him about his father. He looked me deep in the eye and tried his best to be stoic as he told me coldly that he never met his father. A chill went through me as he said it. I could feel the pain behind the words as his mouth retreated into a thin hard line. Now I would never judge a man for what happened to him in his childhood. That's not the point here. The point is that he still carried extreme anguish, shame and anger around his father and hence was a ticking time bomb. I should have gotten out of there ASAP but I gave him a chance and I got to see some more choice red flag behavior (alcohol abuse and extreme negativity) finally ending in him ruining my 31st birthday party and embarrassing me in front of my friends. Don't let it happen to you. Heed the early warning signs.

Why you may have attracted this:

- Have you made peace with and forgiven your father (or mother)? If not, you may attract a man who exhibits the same wounding.

- Do you feel a sense of guilt because you couldn't take

care of your own father, so now you've attracted an un-fathered man to take care of in his place?

- Do you believe that men in general are liars, not trustworthy, hurtful or crazy? That they are non-committal, abusive, destructive or neglectful? His disrespect of his father may mirror your own views about men. The problem here is that because of both of your attention is on how awful men are, he may repeat those very behaviors he claims to detest in his own father.

He's cheap.

A man who begrudgingly spends his money on you will begrudgingly give his heart or time to you as well. It means he either doesn't believe that you or any woman are worthy of his life energy (be it money, love or attention) or that he believes that spending money on you will keep him in lack and poverty. A man should want to provide for you to the best of his ability. As Steve Harvey says, "Know this: It is your right to expect that a man will pay for your dinner, your movie ticket, your club entry fee, or whatever else he has to pay for in exchange for your time" (Harvey 28). This does not mean that we as women are entitled to endless lavish dinners and expensive presents from a man who cannot afford that. But whatever his means are he should be happy to share them with you. Otherwise, he is just not serious about you or willing to take care of any woman at all. In time, you will feel very cheated by giving him your time and attention (and YOUR money, ahem!) and getting very little in return.

Harvey actually goes on to say that it's men that have invented the term "gold-digger" to shame us into thinking that to expect the decency of a chivalrous and paid-for-by-him date is too much to ask for. Don't fall for it. A real man wants to provide and will do everything in his power to do so. "And if a man can't provide, then he doesn't feel like a man, so he flees to escape the horrible feelings of inadequacy, or he's going to bury those feelings in drugs and alcohol. Indeed, you can probably trace a whole host of the pathologies exhibited by the most trifling of men back to their inability to provide" (Harvey 27).

Think of it this way. A man who uses his resources to take care of the women, children and animals in his life is a mature man. A man who thinks the women, children and animals in his life are there for his amusement, is a little boy. (Allen 230).

Why you may have attracted this:

- Do you believe that you're worthy of having someone give you his time, attention and money?

- Did you grow up in a family where you were treated as selfish or yelled at for wanting nice things or even basic things like food and clothes?

- Was your father very controlling of the money in the family and cheap with you or your mother?

- Was your mother an over-giver, and did you grow up watching her do way more for her partner and adult children than was appropriate? Did she put everyone else's needs before her own and is it possible you are repeating those patterns out of habit or loyalty to her?

You met him on the Internet and he won't take down his profile.

OK, so you've been dating someone you met on the Internet. He has told you that he only wants to date you. He calls you his girlfriend and you call him your boyfriend. But he still won't take his Internet dating profile down because he "just wants to let it run out" or "I never check it, it's no big deal" (even though you've checked and you know he was active within the last 24 hours because it says so on the damn site). This says that he is not ready to stop actively looking for potential mates. You met him on a dating site. If he is not looking for other dates, there is no reason for him to be on it. A man who loves you and wants to claim you as his own will gladly remove himself from the site you met him on and make sure that you have done the same. When two people are in the same place in terms of wanting to deepen a relationship, this is automatic and should not even be an issue.

*This happened to me. I was dating a man for 3 months and we were in an exclusive relationship but I noticed that he did not take his *Match.com* profile down and that sometimes it even said that he was active within the last 24 hours. I confronted him on it and told him to either take it down or we would be done. He said that he was just keeping it up because he paid for it and wanted to let it run out. He took it down, but five months later, he ended up breaking up with me because he said that he knew that I was looking to get married and have kids one day and he didn't know if he would ever want that. It was painful as hell and truthfully, the seeds of that breakup were evident in his not taking down his dating profile of his own volition earlier on. I should have seen that one coming. A man who wants to keep you will do everything in his power to prove that he is done with other women.

Why you may have attracted this:

- Yes, it's true you may have attracted this because you don't think you're worthy of a relationship or a man who would want to commit exclusively to you and that is worth exploring within your psyche. Are you so starved for love that you're willing to put up with this half-commitment? Look at that too. But actually, I think this phenomenon of men thinking the next best thing is always just around the corner is VERY common today. Men who are afraid of intimacy just love superficial situations so for them the next best thing actually is around the corner, and around the next corner is the next best thing after that! Internet dating has made it extremely easy for men to date many women. And some men go from woman to woman seeking out the next best thing for years so that they don't have to get real with any of them. So my advice to you in this situation is to give him an ultimatum: get off the site or we're done. And follow through. But even if he takes the profile down to appease you, I would still beware for his wandering eye is may not be limited to one site.

He'll only date you on the weekdays.

This is a sure sign that he's dating a bunch of other women and you are just one of his rotation, which is fine at the beginning. He doesn't really know you and wants to see what you're about. But if you are beyond the 3rd date and you are still relegated to being a weekday girl I'd cut it off. He's obviously not taking you that seriously and you deserve to be with someone who is. Or he's using you just as a plaything to try and have sex with while his REAL social life happens on the weekend with his REAL friends. I repeat, if you're not getting some Friday and Saturday night dates, I would cut it off. (Exceptions: he is legitimately working all weekend and free on weekdays like in the case of emergency room doctors or police officers. Or he has custody of his child all weekend. Of course a man would not introduce you to his child so early on- and actually if he does that's a red flag! But even still, if he is going to seriously date you and he has custody of his child on weekends, he can get a sitter for a Saturday night every so often).

*This happened to me. I was dating a finance guy that I met on eHarmony. We had five dinner and/or movie dates, all during the weekdays, usually Monday or Wednesday. Sexually the furthest I let it get was making out because I could tell he wasn't that serious about me. I did actually like him, but when there was so much time in between our dates and the dates were only on the weekdays, I liked him less and less because it seemed like he wasn't really trying. Of course, he was always "busy" or had friend or work engagements, but let's keep it real; EVERYONE is busy. After the 5th date, he sent me some inane text message that I just ignored and that was the end. I could've cut it off after the 3rd date though when it felt to me that he was making a less than half-hearted attempt to get me.

Why you may have attracted this:

- On the one hand, men do this nowadays. Again with Internet dating it is very easy for a man to date many women at once and I maintain that this is absolutely acceptable because he is probably searching for the one woman who is going to rock his world for the rest of his life and to this man I say, "God bless!" (Also, if he is only looking for sex there are plenty of sites to accommodate those needs nowadays so if you met him in real life or on a serious dating site, it's not likely that he's looking to just sleep with a bunch of women but be careful anyway.) So if this sort of thing has happened to you maybe once or a few times, no big deal. Just cut your loses and move on to someone who is more serious about you.

- On the other hand if you feel like this is consistently happening to you, you want to ask yourself first how much you actually like him (or any of the men you're dating). Maybe you're not that into him and he can feel it. The Universe takes you as seriously as you take It. Are you holding to the standards of what you really want in a partner or are you settling for whatever schmuck will take you out? Do you hold the belief that good men are scarce so you should just take whatever comes your way? Have you made it known to the men taking you out that you are looking for a relationship, or have you made it seem like you are down for whatever? Are you succumbing to the "well at least I get a free dinner" line of thinking? What you do will come back to you and using men for free dinner will come back to bite you as men not taking you seriously (or trying to use you for sex) because any man who is half-aware can feel when he is being used. He may go along with it because you're hot, but there will either be an underlying feeling of resentment or entitlement, neither of which stands to foster a loving relationship.

He doesn't make eye contact with you.

Every woman I've spoken with about this will tell you it's true. A man who cannot make eye contact with you (so much so that you actually notice it) is a red flag. He is either hiding something, has less than chivalrous intentions, is checked out or is dismissive. Some men even blame it on their "ADD." This is bullshit. ADD does not stop a man from looking into the eyes of the woman he cares about or is trying to get to know. The old saying, "the eyes are the windows to the soul" is true. What is he afraid of showing you by looking into your eyes?

*This happened to me. I've actually attracted this red flag twice in my life. And both times, I was on a date with a guy who was telling me that he was open to being in a new relationship if the right person showed up.

As it turned out, both men were "scarred" by their ex-girlfriends, did not want a relationship and were just trying to get in my pants. It's very hard for normal men to look into the eyes of a woman that wants the truth and lie to her. (Sociopaths can do this.) Again, if he avoids eye contact with you so much that you notice it, tread very carefully with this man. Something about him or what he is telling you is not authentic.

Why you may have attracted this:

- Do you want to hear a man's truth, or do you want him to tell you what you want to hear? When you want to hear a man's truth you will, even if you have to read between the lines. Make it your intention to know the truth of every man you go out with.

- Are you hiding something from him? Like attracts like and if you want to get the truth you have to give it as well, even if it's something that puts you in a negative light.

- Are you comfortable looking into a man's eyes? If not, examine why. Are you afraid of what you will find out about him, or yourself? A lot is reflected back to us when we make eye contact with others.

He's rude or unnecessarily angry with the waiter on your dates.

My mother once told me about this red flag and she was absolutely right. On a date, of course a man is going to be nice to you. He's trying to get some! Pay close attention to how he treats the other people on your date, the waiter, the cab driver, the doorman, etc. I've even seen a man be unnecessarily rude to a tarot card reader on our date! These are subordinates because they are on duty and cannot yell back at him and the way he treats them is a window into how he will treat you once you are married to him and "cannot run away." Rude to the waiter/staff is a red flag.

*This happened to me. I was on a date with a man I met on Match.com. He was from the South so I was expecting gentlemanly and chivalrous behavior. And while this man was extremely attentive to me, when the waiter came by to take our drink order (as waiters tend to do) he turned to the waiter and brusquely said: "Excuse me but I'm talking to the lady!" I was immediately turned off; I finished the dinner with as much grace as possible and never spoke to him again.

Why you may have attracted this:

- Were any of your caretakers rage-aholics and is that what you are used to?

- Actually, you may have just attracted this because rude people exist. This may not be your Law of Attraction unless you keep falling for mean and rude guys. The point is that a man should really be on his best behavior at the beginning of a relationship. If he can't contain himself to be polite at the beginning, it's only going to get worse as time goes on. Now if you've been dating a guy for 6 months and he is normally very kind and peaceful but one day completely loses his cool and flips out on the guy working the register at Home Depot, this is not necessarily cause to run. Everyone loses it from time and time and we can cut a man like this some slack. (Trust me, the day will come when you too will lose it and you will want your man to cut you some slack). But these moments of unrestricted rage should be the exception and not the rule.

He doesn't insist or even refuses on wearing a condom when you first start having sex. He doesn't have the STD/pregnancy conversation.

A man that takes himself, you and life seriously will want to protect himself from sexually transmitted diseases (STDs) and unwanted pregnancy. A man who doesn't, is a loose cannon and though he may be a sexy bad-boy, he probably cannot be trusted. If he is not insisting on wearing a condom with you, this is probably what he's doing with any number of women and it's just not safe. Nowadays, the STD statistics are staggering. According to Planned Parenthood, 1 in 4 adults have genital herpes. Every year, up to 1,000,000 people get genital warts (*www.plannedparenthood.org*). One way to prevent STDs like these and others is through proper use of a condom every time you have sex until both partners are tested and know what their sexual health status is. A man who is not concerned about discussing the state of both of your sexual health in this day and age is possibly dangerous or delusional.

(Note: Some guys refuse to wear a condom because when they do they lose their erection. This is a sensitive subject so bring it up gently. But it is no reason whatsoever to put yourself at risk. If he can't wear a condom for whatever reason, I would make sure you see the results of his STD tests AND discuss other birth control options).

This is when waiting to have sex with a man is useful. A man that wants to "hit it and quit it" (who has probably done the same with many other women) will lose interest soon enough when he realizes he's not going to get what he wants that easily and you will be spared from dealing with his ignorance about his sexual health and any consequences of having sex with him.

I understand how frustrating it can be to really want to have sex and physically connect with someone. It is an innate human physical drive and should be treated as normal and not deviant. However, it is well worth the effort to find a sexual partner that is interested in his and your sexual health and is responsible with his body. This is a good sign that he will be responsible with yours as well.

*This happened to me. Twice. Both times, I was on the rebound after a guy broke up with me so I was particularly emotionally vulnerable and I had unprotected sex with the next guy to come along who didn't insist on wearing a condom. By the grace of God, I had no medical repercussions from either incident – just incredible regret and shame. As you can imagine, both guys turn out to be jerks and the signs were present right there in the moment that they didn't insist on having safe sex to protect themselves and me.

In fact, after the breakups that "caused" my rebounds, I felt so unattractive and unworthy, that I felt lucky that anyone even wanted to be with me. And I know I'm not alone in that experience. Ladies, we need to be very careful of the rebound impulse. If you are rebounding to break up the energy of the last man you were with, make sure that your rebound with someone safe that values his own health.

Why you may have attracted this:

- Do you have low self-esteem and believe that you deserve to be treated with disregard?
- Did your parent(s) disregard your health and safety and is that what feels like home to you?
- Do you believe that you are so worthless or unattractive that you are lucky to even have someone that wants you?
- Was your father absent or abusive and having unsafe sex feels fulfilling if only for a night?
- Did you have a rough past including sexual promiscuity and/or alcohol/drug abuse and you think that you are so dirty that no man you interact with will make it worse?

If any of these are true, do not beat yourself up about it. You can get help because these beliefs are more common than you know and most therapists are well trained to deal with them. But to attract a man that loves and cares for your body, you must love and care for yourself and your body first.

His place is an absolute pigsty.

I'm not talking about a few things out of place or some clothes on the floor after a long week at work. That is easily manageable. I'm talking about when you walk in and you are afraid to sit down, or it's hard to make your way through his home because there is so much stuff in the way, or his apartment smells really bad all the time. (Think Hoarders.) These are all signs of a really scattered and cluttered mind and a person who doesn't think they deserve to live in order and peace. How do you think it will be living with him? You can't pick up after him all the time and if he can't have enough thought to pick up after himself (or hire a cleaning lady which is a perfectly acceptable alternative) then you can best believe you may be living in squalor with this man or exhausting yourself preventing it.

The outside is a reflection of the inside. This goes for his personal hygiene and appearance as well. I'm not saying a man has to be ready for a *GQ* photo-shoot at any moment and his apartment should be HGTV-ready, but a man who does not know how to take care of himself and his living space, or doesn't care enough to put himself together to meet a woman, is a red flag. It also shows blatant disregard for your comfort. You clean your apartment when he comes over right? (Please say that you do...) You put yourself together when you know you are going to see him right? (Again, I'm really hoping this is true.) Creating an environment and persona of beauty for one's partner is one of the most wonderful things about being in a relationship and shouldn't be minimized.

Why you may have attracted this:

- First, is your living space a mess or do you walk around looking sloppy? This man may be your mirror.

- Have you lost your desire or ability to dress up and feel sexy like a woman because of challenging life circumstances? Creating beauty for a partner is our responsibility as much as it is theirs. We create beauty in our homes and ourselves because it is pleasing to our partner. Not doing so reflects a lack of excitement of oneself and a lack of interest in how others experience their time with us.

- Do you believe that you deserve to be in a beautiful, clean environment that is pleasing to you?

He is way too into you way too soon in the relationship.

This is likely a seduction to try and have sex with you. Or his intensity about you could be true, but he is probably a guy that is addicted to infatuation. He idealizes women and believes the pedestal that he has put you on is real, but real relationships take staying power. For a brief time you revel in how good it feels to be appreciated that passionately, but like a kid in a candy shop he becomes just as excited about the next new "toy" and becomes bored with the old one (you).

The Don Juan archetype is very well and alive in modern-day dating and he is a scoundrel. A man who is calling you sweetie and baby even before your first date, who is telling you that you are gorgeous, beautiful, amazing, the best woman he has ever met, putting you on a pedestal before he even knows you, stalking you with phone calls and texts, doing his best to talk to you in a seductive voice which is clearly an act; these are all signs that you're dealing with the Don Juan archetype, who wants to bed as many women as possible and then dance off into the night leaving you attached, confused and hurt. He banks on the fact that so many women today are so desperate for love, affection and validation that they will be sucked into this seduction.

Don't get me wrong, you *ARE* beautiful, wonderful, smart, amazing, sexy and everything else he has said. But you are also human. And most likely when this man discovers the parts of you that are not perfect, he will lose interest and leave to find the next "perfect" woman only to dump her too. This is a game you cannot win; unless you really do just want to have sex and fun and when it's over, it's over. But let's be honest, being on the receiving end of this sort of treatment is never fun (OK maybe with the exception of being on vacation, that is a fairly innocent way of having a week-long fling based on infatuation and sex because both parties know it will end after seven days. Except in my experience even this is not as simple as we would like to believe.)

A man that idolizes you is often looking for a savior. When you cannot save him, he will blame you for letting him down and treat you like it's your fault. But let's be real: you can't save another adult, only he can save himself.

*This happened to me. I met a man on *Match.com*. We went for coffee and he seemed nice enough so I took him up on his offer to go to dinner a few nights later. But at the dinner, I could just tell that there was something wrong. He was too effusive in his love for me for as new as our courtship was. He was saying things like, "You're so good I'm never going to let you go. You're perfect." I was creeped-out and just knew something was off with this guy even though I couldn't put my finger on it. Again I finished the dinner with grace but afterward I ended all communication with him, both telephone and online. Then 2 weeks later I got a call from a restricted number. When I answered the phone, a woman said, "This is (his name)'s wife. I saw your number in my husband's phone. How do you know my husband?" Can you imagine my shock as I said, "Um, I met your husband on *Match.com* ..." Two powerful lessons came from this:

1) ALWAYS listen to your gut instinct. You KNOW when something is wrong even if you don't know EXACTLY what is wrong.

2) A man that is way too into you way too soon is most likely a seductive liar or worse.

Another variation of this red flag is a man that buys you expensive presents way too soon in the relationship. Yes you are worth it, but a man that puts too much on the line too soon will be expecting a lot in return whether it's sex or personal sacrifice before you are ready.

Why you may have attracted this:

- On the one hand, men do this. The problem is when you *repeatedly* keep attracting this type of man. And then I would ask the following questions:

- Is there a part of you that is so desperate for love, attention and validation that you are easily sucked into this ruse? Don't feel alone, many women are. A man who really loves you and wants to invest in a relationship will take the time to get to know you and wait to have sex with you. To fill this gaping hole inside yourself, you need to learn to truly love and respect yourself and know that you are worthy of being loved and cherished. How does a grown woman learn to love and respect herself? Well first, she just makes a decision to do so. An affirmation works well here. "I love and accept myself exactly as I am." "I am a loving child of God and I deserve to be loved." Remember there is no outside world; there is only what you project onto the outside world. If your inner state of being is one of love and acceptance then that is what you will receive back. And second, I believe that it is definitely worth doing at least a few sessions with a therapist to explore where the development of a healthy self-esteem may have gone awry. Revisiting these issues as an adult with adult understanding capabilities can really help you re-parent the child within that was not given appropriate love and validation at crucial developmental stages.

- And how do you know when you've truly learned to love and respect yourself? When a man like this withdraws his overly seductive attention and praise (as he most certainly will do because infatuation always has an expiration date) and you are not diminished and still know that you are wonderful and perfect as you are.

- Do you feel the need to save lost men? If so, you'll certainly attract a desperate man who will put the purpose of saving him on you. A more appropriate outlet for this need is to go into the healing arts, either conventional or alternative, and get clients or patients to practice saving. Or better yet, just realize you cannot save your lost father through saving the lost man in front of you. Do what you have to do to make peace with your father instead.

He tells you that he's afraid he's going to hurt you, he's no good for you or that you should run.

Believe it. He's telling the truth. A man who sends you any sort of warning like this is a man you should run away from. You cannot save him. You cannot love him back to wholeness because even HE doesn't believe he can be loved back to wholeness or even worse, he doesn't want to be. He may unconsciously want to remain in the horrible life situation he has created for himself, or just isn't ready to change it yet. In fact, he may never be ready to change it. A man can only let you love him as much as he loves himself. If he doesn't love himself, feel good about himself or think himself worthy of your love, he will reject you and your love at every turn because it feels uncomfortable to him. I don't know ANY woman who got this sort of warning from a man and it turned out to be untrue. And every time, she was kicking herself knowing she could have avoided the unbelievable pain the relationship caused by just having the courage to walk away.

The other reason a man could say all of this is just simply because he knows that he's only looking to get laid and have fun and he can feel that you are most certainly looking for more. He may willfully know that his career is his #1 focus and that you will always take a back seat and he's giving you a chance to get out of something that will surely be unfulfilling to you. My best advice is to listen to him, he's telling the truth. What's worse is that if you don't listen to him, he may lose his respect for you because he can see with plain eyes that you are so needy that you will stand for any sort of treatment. You will never win here. Consider yourself lucky that you got the truth and get out.

I repeat, every man that I've ever met that said this (to either me or my friends) was telling the truth. What's more is that even years later at the time of this publishing, they are ALL still single and have not had committed relationships. A man knows whether he is available or not.

For you, the work here is to accept him as he is. Don't love him for who he COULD be or who you WANT him to be. Accept and see him as he is right now. He is not a bad person; he is simply unavailable. Does he need help? Maybe. But the point is that you need to know that you cannot help him. What you can do is walk away.

Why you may have attracted this:

- Are YOU ready to be truly vulnerable and intimate with someone? A great way to avoid intimacy is to keep attracting unavailable men so that you can blame the lack of emotional connection on them when really it is your pattern because you are terrified of what a man will see if he sees the real you.

- Do you believe you are worthy of being loved? Did your parents tell you or demonstrate to you that you are unworthy of love?

- Was your father a "lost boy" and do you feel guilty that you couldn't save him so you pick other "lost boys" to love and try and save them?

- Was your father absent or unavailable and have you wrongfully adopted the belief that if you were good enough he would have been in your life? Are you still trying to prove that you're "good enough" to your father via the various unavailable men that you date? It was never your job to save your father and you were good enough for his attention the moment you were born. The sooner you can forgive him for not being what you needed him to be, the sooner you will stop attracting lost boys to save.

He's not asking you out on a date.

It's amazing to me how many guys try and slip in the back door these days. You start spending a lot of time with a man a lot and he tells you that he's interested in you and how much he likes you and finds you attractive. (This sort of thing usually happens in the workplace because you spend so much time together but it can happen with any man that you are around frequently). But he's not asking you out. You rationalize that it's because you work together, he's scared, he just got out of a relationship/marriage, he doesn't want to ruin the friendship, he doesn't want to be accused of sexual harassment, etc. The bottom line is, a man that wants to go out with you is going to ask you out. If he's not asking you out, there's a reason. It could be any number of things. It doesn't matter. A man that is professing his love or like to you and not asking you out is a red flag. Don't fall for it. If he asks how he can get close to you, you can respond, "take me to dinner." Great if he does. But if he doesn't, I repeat that there most certainly is a reason that he is holding back. I would not compromise your right as a woman to be courted because he is having an issue with taking you on a date.

*This happened to me. I met a man at work that I was extremely attracted to and the feeling was mutual. We would have daily conversations for 3 hours either in person or on the phone and I was falling in love with him. He said that he couldn't ask me out because he was 6 months divorced and knew that he wasn't ready for a relationship. I should have nipped it in the bud right there but I was falling in love and didn't want to let go. He told me that he couldn't understand why I wanted to be with someone like him that was unavailable. (Another red flag I ignored).

After 6 months of this, I finally slept with him and of course, it changed everything for both of us. Now I felt like he owed me some real respect and attention so I got needy and I'm sure he knew that he crossed a line as well by having sex with a good friend that was in love with him that he knew he had nothing to give to. So I acted like a little girl and started crying and he acted like a little boy and ran away. I also found out later that he was seeing another co-worker of ours and that he was still deeply emotionally entrenched with his ex-wife. I was crushed. I realized that I never really knew this man at all. What I knew and fell in love with was the fantasy of what I made him. And why was it a fantasy? Because we were never out in the real world together and I never got to see the way he responded to things in the world, or the way he would treat me on a date, the way he would talk to my family or what would happen if and when he introduced me to his. His not ever taking me out on a date was unmistakable evidence that he had nothing real to give me, and he knew it.

Dating is the way that we do courtship in our culture nowadays. Yes, it's a formality, but it's an important one. It's the way a man shows you he is willing to invest in you, in a meaningful way, for the long haul. That he cares about your experiences and wants to make some joyful and loving ones for you. Taking you out on a date for private time together in which you can relax and receive is a very important step. Don't let yourself be cheated out of it.

Why you may have attracted this:

- Because there are some serious bull-shitters out there. Don't take it too personally. It happens. Women sometimes attract men who are just testing the water to see how far they can get with without having to really invest. As soon as you require these guys to take you out or leave you alone, they will most certainly step up to the plate or fall away. It's up to you to draw the line in the sand and not be so needy as to get your emotional needs met from a man who has no intention of creating the space for something real with you.

He talks about women (or his ex's) in a disrespectful way, like they are "bitches" or "crazy."

How long do you think it's going to take until those judgments are thrown at you? If he's made up his mind that women are crazy bitches, not long at all. Another red flag is a man who will use the word "cunt" when talking about a woman. This is not just crass; it's a sign of an underlying misogyny. When he talks about some or all of his ex-girlfriends, are they crazy too? Do you really believe they're all crazy? Did he have to file a restraining order against one of them? Maybe it's time to consider what role he played to make them that crazy. I'm not saying that some women are not crazy, but it takes two to tango and *generally*, when a woman is treated with honesty and integrity, she does not go bananas on a man.

*This happened to me. One of my ex-boyfriends described his ex-girlfriend as crazy and needy. Except after the way he treated me, I can see exactly why she became that way!

If the pattern of women in his life is one of unstable insanity, watch out. You could actually be with a crazy-maker.

Why you may have attracted this:

- Do you distrust women yourself?

- Have you healed your relationship with the primary feminine energy in your life, you mother or female caretaker?

- Have you taken the time to create a peaceful, non-crazy existence for yourself including: quiet time or mediation, healthful eating, joyous exercise, loving friendships, and responsible handling of your finances? If you haven't, when this guy throws the "crazy" label at you, you are likely to believe him.

- Are you addicted to stimulants like caffeine,

sugar, cocaine, speed or other legal or illegal drugs that are actually making you crazy and is this man a mirror reflecting this crazy-making addiction back to you?

He's not over his ex.

You can generally tell if this is the case quite soon. Either he will flat out tell you (as some guys have done with me) or you'll see the way he broods over her and recounts a little too much of how much she hurt him. When you are in a relationship, it is obviously okay to talk about your relationship past, but if your guy is dwelling on it, he is not over it.

This is especially true if he "hates" her and is saying unkind things about her. Whatever he is accusing her of doing or being, it is likely that those very same accusations will be thrown at you one day because he has not healed from what happened.

*This happened to me. I once met a good-looking guy on *Match.com* who was a personal trainer, just like me, and I thought we'd have a lot in common. On our first date, he told me in extreme detail about how when he met his ex-girlfriend's parents, she lied and told them that he was just a friend because she didn't think they would accept him as her boyfriend. I could tell that he was still very hurt from their breakup so when he didn't call me for a 2nd date, I just let it go.

About a year later, I must have ended up in his online search on *Match.com* again because he reached out to me on the site. He took me out on another first date. All in all this date was much better and lasted 8 hours. He met me at the gym to work out, then we went for dinner at a nice seafood restaurant, then we walked around Greenwich Village finally ending up at a Starbucks and having coffee until he walked me home and kissed me. Actually, this time I really was upset and surprised that he didn't call me for a 2nd date. But I remember when I was at the seafood restaurant with him, he told me the whole story AGAIN about how his ex-girlfriend introduced him to her parents as a friend, except this time the story had gathered even MORE momentum and he gave me even more details. This man that had not released her one bit since I had last gone out with him.

So how long does it take a man to get over an ex? It's different for everyone. Ask him where he is with the whole thing and what he is looking for and do not have sex with him until you are sure that he is telling you the truth. Listen with your instinct, not just your ears. In the past, I've asked men, "Are you ready to trust someone again?" The answer to that question usually tells you everything you need to know.

Why you may have attracted this:

- Are you over your ex? It was amazing to me how many times I attracted a man who was still attached to someone else when I was actually attached to an ex of mine.

He needs to be drunk/high every time he sees you. Or he's an active drug or alcohol abuser.

This man cannot enter a loving and committed relationship. If he can't be with you sober and in the light of day for all to see, he can't love you. He is terrified of true intimacy and terrified of himself. He is scared that you will see the real him and numbs out with substances because he hates himself. If he hates himself, he will not be able to let you love him. This is a man who has not worked out his inner demons and they will surface at some point. Perhaps it would be a good idea if you left him to work it out instead of having him come to a personal crisis when you're already knee deep in a marriage with kids with this guy?

What he needs is help. Not your help, but professional help. There are plenty of 12 step programs all over the world with a high success rate for helping people with addiction, or helping the people who love addicts. You have no control over a man's drug use. This is up to his discretion alone. What you can do is let him know that you love him, but that you cannot tolerate the drug use and will not be with him until he gets help. If you overlook it, you are enabling the dysfunction and will have to deal with the consequences later. An addict is not in control of his behavior and needs help beyond your love. Your love and unconditional acceptance may be part of his healing, but it is not enough to do the job completely. If you are struggling with this, get to an Al-Anon meeting yourself.

Why you may have attracted this:

- Were either of your parents alcoholics/drug users and the only time they paid any attention to you (positively or negatively) was when they were drunk or high?

- Does part of you believe that you are a horrible person and if a sober person with real awareness were to come into your life, they would quickly leave because they would soon realize how awful you are?

- Do you have a need for the man in your life to be dependent or co-dependent on you because you believe he will leave otherwise?

- Do you have the need to control and so you attract out-of-control men who need your leadership?

He has a bad case of TMI.

This is a red flag when it happens too early on. TMI (too much information) is when a guy tells you way too much about himself way too quickly. You can tell its TMI when you feel uncomfortable with the rate that he has disclosed extremely personal information about himself or his family. This will be different for every guy (and every woman's comfort zone) but if someone is telling you deep dark family secrets on the first or second date, that is generally considered TMI. The reason this is a problem is because a man should want you to know that he is a chivalrous, kind, intelligent and protective gentleman before he lets you in on the things about him that are less than dignified or even embarrassing. Letting you in on his awful drama or wounds too early on is usually a sign that he defines himself by his wounds as opposed to defining himself by his resilience to overcome the trauma that has occurred in his life. It can also be a sign that what he's really looking for is support and help, not a romantic relationship. Everyone has been through trauma and I believe that two people should deeply share the things that have happened in their lives, but there is an appropriate time for this. It's after both people have established themselves as an otherwise emotionally stable and secure adult.

For people that are terrified of intimacy, TMI is a great way to sabotage the prospect of ever having it. It's sort of like, "I will show you how crazy I am from the beginning so that if you reject me I can blame it on you and say that you just couldn't handle me." This can be hard because if you are sensitive enough you can usually feel the person dying inside to connect with someone beneath the huge ego on the outside that is pushing you away. It's really up to that person whether they are going to choose to let you in or not. Be present with him and you will be able to determine if you are going to be able to make a connection; that is, if you want to. At the beginning dating is supposed to be fun, you don't want to feel like an unpaid therapist or like you're watching an after-school special.

In her book *Daring Greatly*, researcher Brene Brown calls TMI "Floodlighting" and says that it's a shield to prevent the person using it from engaging in true vulnerability. Floodlighting is when one shares a shame story with another person with whom they have not yet developed "connectivity", as in a man that you are on a first or second date with. You hear a story that was WAY too personal for how little you know this man and you feel like a floodlight has been shone in your eyes. You emotionally (and perhaps physically) want to wince and recoil. "When it's over, we feel depleted, confused, and sometimes even manipulated" [Brown

160]. Brown says, "the intentions behind this kind of sharing are multifaceted and often include some combination of soothing one's pain, testing the loyalty and tolerance in a relationship, and/or hot-wiring a new connection." (As in "Yes this is our first date but I'm going to share this and you'll think I'm being vulnerable and want to be my girlfriend/have sex with me") [Brown 159].

Don't fall for it, and don't feel sorry for him. Regardless of what he has been through, an emotionally stable man wants you to feel safe with him and will not bulldoze you with shame stories before your relationship has reached a certain level in which they are appropriate.

*This happened to me. I met a guy at a New Year's Eve party. We kissed when the ball dropped and it certainly had the makings of a romantic beginning. That is until he drove me home and recounted to me a story about this girl that he met in a club back in his hometown in New Jersey. She was from out of town and she was very pretty. She told him that she was looking for her father. Apparently, she and her sister were conceived from an extra-marital affair and their father told their mother (who was the other woman) that he wanted nothing to do with them. Their mother had since passed away and for a while, the girls suffered through the foster care system. They reached out to their biological father for help and he was ignoring them so they were in town trying to find him.

He wished her all the best with her search. They were really hitting it off and he decided to take her back to his place at the end of the night. Right before they were about to become intimate, he asked her, "so what's your father's name?" and almost died when she said his father's name. He was about to hook-up with his half sister!

This was not exactly a first meeting type of story. This guy had serious misjudgments about boundaries and propriety. I felt uncomfortable hearing this story. The red flag was further validated by the fact that the next words out of his mouth were, "So are you one of those girls that I have to take to dinner a few times before I hit it?" I replied, "Nope, I'll save you the effort," and I never saw him again.

Why you may have attracted this:

- Do you have a bad case of TMI? (I'll admit that I did. But I promise you this guy cured me of it once I learned what it felt like to be on the receiving end.)

- Do you define yourself by your wounds instead of your resilience to overcome those traumas?

- Are you afraid of intimacy and do you use TMI to push people away? Or do you use Floodlighting to try and force an emotional connection?

- Are you a rescuer, always looking for a victim to save?

He's told you he's not looking for a relationship. He says that he doesn't ever want to get married.

He means it. He's not looking for a relationship and there's a 99.9% chance that you will not change that. If this is not OK with you, tell him your feelings and leave him alone.

This really is an important question to ask early on, like within the first 3 dates. If you ask and remain calm and really want to hear the truth, he will tell you. Some men are not the marrying type and don't wish to practice monogamy. Be glad that he's at least honest about it.

Women are often afraid to ask these questions or truthfully admit that they'd like to be in a committed relationship or married. I think this is a grave mistake. The only man who would be turned off by you asking what he's looking for in a relationship or telling him what you're looking for, is a man who is either not into you or not into being in a relationship period. His truth can either come out at the beginning if you ask him, or later on because you were afraid to ask. But it's quite likely it will be the exact same truth.

Admitting that you are looking for a relationship is not needy. Demanding that HE be the partner that you're looking for, now THAT is needy. But stating your desires and remaining open to hear about his desires are what vulnerability and honesty are all about. If you don't have the honesty to openly discuss what each partner wants within the first few dates, then there is no way there's enough maturity to sustain a long-term relationship.

Why you may have attracted this:

- You're female and dating – that's why. The problem is not in meeting these guys because everyone is entitled to be honest about what they're looking for. The problem is if he tells you the truth and you think it will change because of you. It won't. Or if he tells you the truth and you know that you really want to be in a relationship and continue with him anyway and settle for a sort of half-relationship. Don't lie to yourself. You'll only be hurt in the end.

He tries to push his sexual agenda way too early. (Also known as: he invites to you to come over to cook, watch a movie or see his apartment when you barely know him).

A man who is looking for a relationship will take the time to build one and develop emotional intimacy with a woman first. Of course, there are exceptions to this rule as evidenced by the couples that ended up getting married after having sex on the first night. But these are the exception not the rule. A good guy will understand that a woman may not feel comfortable being alone in an apartment with a man she barely knows.

A man who does not respect your right to take the sexual part of the relationship slowly is not interested in being in an emotionally connected relationship. In all fairness, as a man he may not know how to develop emotional intimacy and may always rely on the woman to initiate that sort of closeness. And that's fine. As women, that is primarily our job. But if he is not respecting your wishes to take the sexual part of the relationship slowly, he is not a protective fully-grown man; he is a little boy having a hissy fit because he can't get his way. A real man puts your feelings before his own and will want you to feel comfortable and safe with him. That means going at your speed sexually.

Why you may have attracted this:

Men do this. Men want to have sex. Period. It's not so much that you attracted it. (Hey, you're probably a sexy, desirable babe. Take it as a compliment.) But what are you going to do now? Know that you will not rope a man into an intimate relationship with hot sex. For men, sex is sex and love is love and the two may possibly intertwine but don't necessarily have to.

Why Men Want Sex and Women Need Love explains why this is possible. Findings in studies done by professors Raquel and Ruben Gur at the University of Pennsylvania School of Medicine show:

> ...that the anterior commissure, which connects the left and right brain hemispheres, is 12% smaller in men than in women and that the corpus callosum — the cord that lets one brain hemisphere exchange information with the other — has up to 30% fewer connections in men than in women...This gives men their 'one-thing-at-a time' approach to everything they do and is why they can focus more intensely on single tasks than women. Having a 'monotracking' brain lets men focus intently on either sex or love. Sex can be just sex, and love can be just love — and occasionally they happen together. This allows men to do something that women don't understand: have sex with women they don't like (Pease 181).

"Men can easily compartmentalize sex into a simple act like shaving — after you've had a shave, you don't think about it again till the next time." (Pease 182). But as women we know that this is not true for us, there is an emotional component when we have sex. Sex and love (or at least like) usually happen together. And even if a woman has decided that she's just going to have casual sex with a man and convince herself that she doesn't care about him, let her see that man walking with another woman a few days after they've had sex and we'll see how much she doesn't really care. Even the most stoic of women will feel this. So, don't fool yourself into thinking that you will get a guy to like you by acquiescing to his sexual advances. This is not the way men work. However, if you have sex with a man before you know how you feel about him and the sex is good, there's a good chance that you'll fall for him because oxytocin, the hormone released with orgasm, is also the bonding hormone. You will become emotionally attached to a man who made love to you well, so be careful and take the time to make sure this is someone you WANT to become attached to.

For me this means that I'm not going over to a man's apartment or having him over to mine until I know him really well. And to be perfectly honest, I have a pretty, strong sex drive so I make sure that I'm not alone with a man in one of our homes unless I'm ready to be sexual with him. You never make sound decisions in the heat of the moment, so why put yourself there if you're not ready.

He is effeminate or has homoerotic tendencies.

This is not a red flag if it's alright with you. Some women are comfortable dating primarily feminine-energy and/or bisexual men. The truth is there are no hard and fast rules about what is even considered effeminate and/or homoerotic. The only problem here is when you keep attracting men that you experience as effeminate and you don't want to. Do you feel like you keep going out with men whom you're quite sure will come out of the closet one day?

Why you may have attracted this:

Ask yourself the following questions:

- "Am I afraid of sexual attention from a masculine-energy man?"

- "Is my behavior toward masculine men castrating?"

- "Do I have derogatory attitudes about masculine men?"

- "Do I have unrealistic expectations about what a straight man should want to like or do or how a straight man should act?" (For example: if you're looking for a straight guy who loves yoga, karaoke and going to the ballet, you may be looking for a LONG time...)

If the answer to any of these questions is "Yes" then you may want to examine your attitudes more deeply because they are manifesting in the men you attract.

He hides behind technology.

We have unlimited ways of getting in touch with each other today which is wonderful and convenient. But nothing takes the place of in person, or at least by phone or Skype, human interaction. Not wanting to talk to you on the phone or Skype is a red flag. Some men are not phone gabbers like women and that is totally fair. But if that is the case then he should make the effort to get to know you in person and procure ample opportunities to have quality face time with you.

With today's work, school and family schedules, many people do not have unlimited time to date as frequently as possible to get to know each other. I believe speaking on the phone or Skype can be a real way to continue connecting when schedules don't allow. But do not get caught up in the endless, half-assed, text message conversations that are so prevalent today. This is not a way to build intimacy. Maybe some guys know that. They give you just enough attention to get you hooked, without giving of their hearts and souls in any real way. A man who will not speak to you on the phone or Skype will not be ready to give of himself, especially when he brings up major issues by text or instant message. This is a sign of a coward and a hider. Red flag indeed!

Text messages are great for staying connected when you physically cannot speak by phone. But without sufficient voice-to-voice time they are not enough to build a relationship.

*This happened to me. I met a guy at work once, a client of one of my colleagues who expressed interest in me. He was good-looking and had a great job in finance so I told my colleague to give the guy my number. He texted me to make plans and I suggested that he call me so that we could discuss it. (I purposely wanted to see if he would call me because even though texting is so common nowadays, I absolutely hate being demanded by text message to show up at some random location with a person I hardly know. Way more charming to actually call.) A few days later, he called me and we set up the plans and at the end of our brief 10-minute conversation he said, "you know I have to tell you, I'm not really a phone guy. I don't like talking on the phone so how about we just text from now on." I decided to give it a chance. I figured maybe this guy would make up for his lack of wanting to talk on the phone with frequent in person dates or sweet text messaging. Nope. It was actually an early red flag as to the level of his fear of intimacy. A guy who wants you in his life will give you the green light to call, text, email, snail mail, Skype, scream from outside his window, etc. He will let you know if he wants you around. For the duration of the time that I dated this guy, he always held me at arm's length. And the signs were present right in that very first conversation.

And as for sexting…it's a red flag when a man you just met sends you a naked picture of himself. A man who is going to take you seriously is not sending naked pictures before he knows you well enough. And if he requests a naked or overly sexual picture of you before he is your boyfriend, run for the hills. I know this is common nowadays, but if you are looking for a relationship, you just cannot go there. Once you are in a relationship with someone, sexting is okay as long as you trust that your images are not going to be thrown up on some website.

Why you may have attracted this:

- Do you believe you are worthy of a man's full attention without the prospect of him having sex with you immediately?

- Do you believe you are interesting and engaging to talk to? If you don't, then a man will most likely treat you that way.

- Are you so desperate for the scraps of someone's time and attention that you will stand for this behavior?

- Do you hide behind technology? Are you afraid of true intimacy and vulnerability?

- (And as for why you attracted the sexting – because we live in a crazy world. Don't take it too personally. It's not you – it's *HIM*!)

He asks to borrow/have money.

Oh yeah, this is not cool. Now I'm not talking about once you're married, because at that point it is implied that you will be sharing assets. But a man that asks to borrow money too early on (even if you are wealthy) is a red flag.

Dr. Pat Allen refers to this type of guy as having the "Peter Pan Syndrome." We all know the song "I Won't Grow Up" from that play and that's basically what we're dealing with here. A Peter Pan never got enough love in childhood and is still waiting for "Mom" to come in and take of or rescue him. So perhaps at the beginning, he'll reel you in by taking you out on nice dates and laying the charm on thick. (Even little boys know how to play the game to get what they want). But within 4-8 weeks, his generosity will dry up and he'll start asking you for money, favors and the right to crash at your place before any of this is appropriate

(Allen 231). (Which is why I suggest that you do not have sex with him until you've been dating him for 2 months. Very few men can keep the act up longer than this and you'll have a much better idea of what you're dealing with- either a truly chivalrous and protective man, or a Peter Pan dressed up as that man).

In fact:

> A man like this can turn a relationship into a nightmare because usually, after his generous period ends, he will shut down and become passive-aggressive, often deliberately provoking you into begging for him to give you what you want. Little boys love weird women. He sees no problem in driving you crazy, and although you may have been reasonably sane when he met you, he will train you to become weird by pushing you away, then pulling you close again, all within a very short period of time.

> So what do you do if you find yourself in such a relationship? You could scream, eat, drink, take drugs or work obsessively, but I suggest that you say, "I really appreciate what a great guy you are, but I'm not very comfortable here. I'll probably be leaving for the weekend, or permanently." (Allen 231).

*This happened to me. I was dating a much younger cyclist and after four dates, he had the nerve to ask me (text me actually) for $200 to buy a part to fix his bike for competitions. He was 21 years old at the time. He had 2 parents, 3 siblings, many cousins and his teammates all to ask for money, but he asked me. This is totally inappropriate. When I said no, I never heard from him again. Shocker.

I've heard of other women paying for guys' tuition, letting them live at their home rent-free or bailing them out financially when life gets crazy. I've also heard about women who come from wealthy families being expected by their guys to pay for all of their dates. I promise you a real man would never do this. A real man will want to take care of you and while some sharing of financial responsibility is appropriate, a man that allows you to pay for things he should pay for on his own is a little boy and you are his mother. Let him go and allow him to grow up so that one day he can be a man to someone instead of continuing to enable his man-child behavior. Even if a man makes less money than you, a real man will want to pay for dates within his means and provide for you the best way he can.

Why you may have attracted this:

- Do you believe you have anything of value to give to your man besides money, like your heart, your love and your support?

- Do you believe that men are little children that will never grow up?

- Do you believe you can make a man love you by financially taking care of him?

- Do you believe that you are not good enough to get a man who wants you, so you have to take on a man who NEEDS you so he won't leave you?

- Do you feel guilt about the wealth that has been bestowed upon you in life, perhaps wealth that you didn't specifically create but was given to you through your family? If you feel guilty about having money, you will certainly manifest a leech to take it from you.

- Do you like being in control and to use your money to control a man? This is the best way to emasculate him and ultimately lose him once he puts himself together and is no longer dependent on you.

He's married.

Yes I know he's told you his wife is a total bitch and he doesn't want to divorce her and lose his money (it's cheaper to keep her), he's staying for the kids, he just needs more time, blah, blah, blah. He's really in love with you and you guys have an amazing connection but he's just stuck in a situation right now... Bullshit. He's not leaving her. And he's jerking you around.

A real man will handle the responsibilities of his life and honor his commitments. A man-child will blame his life on everyone around him including his wife and sneak around to get his needs met no matter how dishonest he's being. If he is an adult and the commitment that he made to his wife no longer serves him or speaks to the highest truth of who he is he will divorce her. It's that simple. If he is not divorcing her but is cheating on her, he is a child. And what is cheating? It's lying and dishonestly breaking a commitment. And it is likely that one day he will do the same to you. In the words of Oscar Wilde, "A man who marries his mistress leaves a vacancy in that position."

Why is he doing this? It's quite simple. He can. You are allowing it. And, to some degree, you have to wonder if she knows and has just decided to stick her head in the sand but perhaps she does not know. He's made his wife his mother. She manages his house, cooks, takes care of his kids, does his laundry or is the trophy on his arm and he has possibly de-sexualized her and needs a sexual outlet...you. And maybe this is exciting for a hot minute. But it will become nauseating and soul eroding with enough time.

It is likely he is invested in the Madonna-whore view of women. The Madonna-whore complex, first identified by Sigmund Freud, is when a man sees women as either saintly Madonnas or slutty whores and cannot maintain sexual arousal within a committed, loving relationship. He has chosen a woman to be his wife that he sees as exhibiting the qualities of the Madonna, patient, nurturing and pure. Once they are married and especially after the birth of their first child, he will no longer see his Madonna-wife as a sexual being. He doesn't want to tarnish the sanctity and purity of their relationship so he seeks out "whores," women he perceives as dirty or debased, to fulfill his sexual gratification (and in essence punish). Freud theorized that this usually happens to men who grew up with a cold, distant or unavailable mother. These men often seek out mates who are similar in personality to their mothers to try and fulfill unmet childhood emotional needs. They then become sexually turned off because no man wants to have sex with his mother. So he seeks out extra-marital affairs to fulfill this need (*http://www.askmen.com*).

I hate to state the obvious, but in this scenario, you are the whore, which makes it unlikely that you ever be the wife. You will always the side-girl, sex plaything, because no man wants a woman that he perceives as a whore as a wife. This type of man does not understand that all women have aspects of both the Madonna and the whore in them. Just as he cannot see his wife as a sexual being, he cannot see you as a nurturing woman that deserves committed love. Putting up with this behavior shows him that you do not believe you are worthy of more. And if his wife really does treat him awfully, on some level he believes he deserves it. (If his mother treated him the same way his wife does you need to look no further for answers). This man doesn't love himself and won't be able to let you love him either.

Some couples today have open relationships and have agreed to allow one or both partners get their sexual needs met outside of the relationship. This is not lying if it is the agreed upon arrangement between spouses. If you want to get involved with such a man, first make sure that he is telling the truth and second, do so only if you are looking for a fling or some fun. Have no illusions that he will leave his wife for you.

*This happened to me. And it is why I have such strong opinions about it. I've been that sad chick on the side. And I promise you nothing I have ever been involved in eroded my self-esteem or crushed my spirit as badly as that experience.

I was 27 and he was 40. He was a good-looking, charismatic personal trainer that worked with me. I would catch him checking me out from time to time but I knew he was married so I never paid it any mind. I had heard through the grapevine that his marriage was on the rocks. One day at work, he asked me out and I assumed that he must have been separated from his wife.

On our date, I asked him if he was separated or getting divorced and he told me that he wasn't. I asked why he asked me out and he said it was because he liked me. I told him that I couldn't proceed with a married man. We finished dinner and he drove me home. He knew that he was about to lose me so he made a desperate move and kissed me and began telling me how special he thought I was and how he stares at me at work all the time and can't stop thinking about me. And I fell for it hook, line and sinker. Why? On the surface, it was because I was lonely. There wasn't an abundance of great guys coming after me. (In hindsight, I realize that when I was in my 20's, I pushed plenty of good guys away for stupid reasons. I had been hurt so much in my life that I guarded myself from true intimacy with any man. I didn't love myself and I couldn't imagine someone really loving and accepting me exactly the way I was). This guy was saying words of affirmation and validation that I never heard from my own father. According to my therapist, John McMullin, we get inspiration from our mother (or the feminine role model in our life) and validation from our father (or masculine role model in our life). A woman who is not validated by her own father (like me) will give away her power to men who validate her. And so I felt like I couldn't walk away from this married man because "no one else could understand me" and "no one else could love me."

Now if like me, you didn't have a father that validated how worthy of love you are, it does not mean that you are doomed. It does mean that part of your maturity as a woman and the road to reclaiming your own power will be in learning to validate and re-parent yourself. Part of this process is in learning to forgive your father for what he could not be. My own father was never validated by his father, and his mother enabled his dependence on her and his failure to emotionally mature. My father was uncomfortable around women in general and did not know how to functionally relate to me. Not to mention, I wasn't the easiest daughter to deal with. I see how he could have felt uneasy putting himself out there to develop a closer relationship with me.

When you understand your pattern from childhood and stand up to validate yourself as a woman who is worthy of love, you will no longer fall prey to the emotional manipulations of unavailable men.

This was the only way I knew to get my emotional needs met. I stayed in this awful situation for a year, and it almost destroyed me. You need to figure out why you are allowing this. But first, run. Consult a therapist immediately.

Why you may have attracted this:

- During your childhood, did you feel that you were trying to win your father's attention away from your mother? Did you feel that your father didn't love you and it was your mother's fault? In some way, are you still trying to get back at your mother? Your married love interest's wife is now metaphorically your mother.

- Growing up did you constantly feel that you had to compete for and win your father's love from your other siblings?

- Do you believe that there's not enough good men

to go around so you must do whatever you can to snag or steal one?

- Do you believe that all men are liars and cheaters? Congratulations, you've attracted exactly what you believe.

- Are you so desperate for love and attention that you are willing to settle for the scraps of someone else's life and time?

- Do you believe that you are worthy of your own relationship?

- Do you believe that someone could fully love you exactly the way you are? Can you love a man exactly the way he is, faults and all? Having an affair is a great way to have a sort of pseudo-intimacy with a man. You don't really have to be vulnerable and risk anything because he's not really available. So you can tell him all of your deep, dark secrets and have crazy wild sex with him because you're not afraid of him leaving you because he's not even yours to begin with. Affairs are a sneaky and psychologically damaging way of avoiding intimacy because you are tricked into believing that you are being intimate and close with someone. But intimacy is based on truth and happens in the light of day as well.

DATING FOR ABOUT 6 MONTHS

You've seen his imperfections and he's seen yours

"Relationships — easy to get into, hard to maintain. Why are they so hard to maintain? Because it's hard to keep up the lie. 'Cause you can't get nobody being you. You got to lie to get somebody. You can't get nobody looking like you look, acting like you act, sounding like you sound. When you meet somebody for the first time, you're not meeting them. You're meeting their representative." –Chris Rock

You've been going out for a while (over 6 months) and he introduces you to people he knows by your first name, instead of giving you a title.

I actually got this one from Steve Harvey's book *Act Like a Lady, Think Like a Man* and it's totally spot on. A man who cares about you and is planning on investing in you will let everyone in his life know that you are his girlfriend (fiancé, wife, life partner, etc.). If he is not serious about you, he will say this is my friend or this is "your name". Its time to evaluate what you think is going on in this relationship and compare it with what he thinks is going on. Because if he is not introducing you to people with a title, you are not in his plans for his future, no matter how he behaves when the two of you are alone. It's that simple (Harvey 21).

Also, it's good to watch how he behaves when you call him your boyfriend. Does he look like he enjoys it, or does he squirm? A man that's sticking around with serious intentions will LOVE it.

He's a mama's boy.

Yes, you want to be with someone who loves, respects and helps his mother but there is a limit. When a son becomes an adult, a mother should naturally let go and let him develop deep emotional attachments to romantic interests. A mama's boy is a man whose mother became overly emotionally entrenched with him at a young age. She was probably missing an appropriate man to get her needs met (as in a boyfriend or husband of appropriate age) and inappropriately got her needs met from her son. (This is even possible if she was married but her husband was checked out and she then turned to her son for emotional sustenance.) So the first step is to realize where this is coming from and have some compassion for her and what she has been through. Hating her and blaming her will only make it worse because she is a woman in pain and the backlash will come at you hard. Can you forgive her and love her? If so, you are on the path to healing this situation.

It makes a man feel extremely powerful to know that his mother's happiness lies in his hands. (Now we know her happiness does not lie in his hands. No adult's happiness is the responsibility of another. This is the false dynamic set up between this man and his mother.) Once you have forgiven and chosen to have compassion for his mother, you must communicate your feelings to him. Give him feedback and give him a chance to respond and correct the behavior. A man that wants to keep you will include you in his family and make it known to his mother that you are important to him.

But if he does not change the behavior, this is most certainly a red flag. Do not think it will get better with time or once you marry him. A man needs to be ready to claim his emotional independence from his mother and his right to make some special lady the center of his life. If he can't get this right in the dating and courtship period of your relationship do not move forward with this man. Most likely, you will always play second fiddle to his mother.

Why you may have attracted this:

- Do you feel like you competed with your mother for your father's love? If so, this may be that situation dropping into your life at a new level. Heal the initial wound and you will begin to heal the current manifestation of that wound.

- Do you feel that there is a lack of love in the world in general, that there's not enough love to go around?

- Do you feel that you are worthy of being the #1 woman in a man's life? If you are going to love, honor and support him then you are certainly entitled to that slot.

He's not interested in fulfilling you sexually.

This is sort of like being cheap but even worse.

I understand that not every man is blessed with a natural sexual prowess. Every woman is different and for a man, it can be challenging to figure out what pleases a woman and turns her on. And that's just fine. But a man that cannot get over his ego to concern himself with learning to please you sexually will probably be checked out and selfish in the rest of your life with him.

Where does this behavior come from? He may think that women are not interested in sex, are dirty if they experience sexual pleasure, or that he is somehow degrading himself to please a woman. There may be some low-level hatred of women or unresolved mommy issues here. Or more innocently, most men have been watching porn since they were 13 and now incorrectly believe that the majority of women like rough sex. The pornography industry is geared mostly toward the male customer and is all about male pleasure; filmed largely by unhappy men that can't get laid, for unhappy men who can't get laid. So most men have no context in which to figure out what a woman likes sexually. There are men out there who are eager to learn what turns you on but the only way to know if you're dealing with one is to tell him. This means that you yourself need to have a good idea of what turns you on and be open, vulnerable and confident enough to share it with him.

My favorite sex columnist, Dan Savage, uses a term called "GGG" which stands for "good, giving, and game," which is what we should all strive to be for our sex partner and what he should strive to be for us. Think "good in bed," "giving equal time and equal pleasure," and "game for anything—within reason." When one's partner is not "GGG" and interested in giving pleasure as much as receiving, Savage frequently gives the advice to "DTMFA" – "dump the motherfucker already." And I have to agree with him.

Why you many have attracted this:

- Do you believe that sex is dirty and shameful and as such, that you do not deserve to be fulfilled? If so, you will certainly attract a partner who agrees.

- Do you believe that you are not deserving of pleasure in general? That you are so worthless that you're lucky enough to have someone paying attention to you (if only for 15-30 minutes at a time) so why rock the boat and ask for more?

- Do you believe that you are too fat or unattractive to be deserving of loving sexual attention? (Let's be real ladies. LOTS of women, who some would judge as fat or unattractive are happily married and having great sex. Don't delude yourself. You don't need plastic surgery, you need an attitude adjustment.)

- Do you know what you like as a woman and have you tried to communicate that to your partner in a loving and non-threatening way?

- Are you making an effort to satisfy him? *A Course in Miracles* says, "Only what you are not giving can be lacking in any situation." You want hot sex? Then bring it sweetie!

He has a child or children that he doesn't see or take care of.

Major red flag. I don't care how much his child's mother is a "bitch"; a real man will fight to see his own children. Wild horses and tsunamis could not keep a real man from his kids. In fact, it is against the law to keep a child from his/her biological parent. This is kidnapping! A real man will do whatever it takes to be a part of his child's life.

Know this: if he will not fight for his own children, his flesh and blood, he will never fight for you. He is not capable of being the committed man you need. I know there are extenuating circumstances in this area but think about this: if a woman will not let a man see his kids, what did he do to her? (This is not always true, but we can imply that there was some deal of disrespect towards her if she will not let him see his kids). Get the facts before you proceed with this man. He may or may not treat you any differently than he treated his child's mother unless he has done some serious healing and inner work.

*This happened to me. I met a guy that I really liked. I found him extremely attractive and we had a lot in common. I knew that he had one son with an ex-girlfriend and that he and she had a peaceful parenting relationship.

Once we started getting closer, he told me that he had another son with a different woman except he had no relationship with this son. When I asked "why" he said it was because she wouldn't tell him where she and the child were living. He made her sound vindictive and horrible. I believed his story.

As the months passed, more details came out about what happened. When she got pregnant, they weren't in a relationship and this guy didn't believe it was his child so he made her do a paternity test. After the paternity test proved he was the father, he still wasn't good about paying child support so she withdrew the child from this guy's life. Also, baby mama #1 and baby mama #2 were in contact and their sons knew each other, yet this guy was estranged from child #2. Hmm, now how could that be?

I don't know what was going on in this woman's head because I do not know her. However, this guy turned out to be a total liar and treated me horribly. Now that we are no longer dating, I refuse to speak with him because he hits below the belt so to speak. He is dishonest and tries to insert himself back into my life but has no intention of following through with me. He is downright mean, a textbook mind-fucker. I've actually had to block him on my phone. Thank GOD I have no children with him because I get to cut the cord with him forever. What I learned from this experience is that if a woman refuses to let a man see his children, you must dig deeper before you engage with him. I promise you, everything is not kosher. I don't know the full extent of what he did to her, but if it was anything like the way he treated me I can understand why she cut him out of her life.

Why you may have attracted this:

- Did your own father bail on you? Many times our primarily male relationship is played out in our adult relationships.

- Are you rationalizing this man's behavior because you are getting from him the validation that you didn't get from your own father? Actually, the problem here is not attracting a man who is not seeing his child(ren). The real problem is when you rationalize this behavior and find it acceptable.

He is physically abusive to you.

This is an absolute red flag. A man who hits you, or has admitted to hitting other women, will continue to be an abuser unless he gets help. I do believe a man can be healed of this, but only if he works with a qualified therapist. If he hits you and is not willing to get help, walk away immediately and if you fear for your safety contact the authorities. (Also, if he is just beginning to get help for this problem chances are he will need some time to break the pattern. Do not allow yourself to continue to be physically abused while he is "healing." Get out. Allowing yourself to be abused will destroy your self-esteem.)

Men who are physical abusers generally came from families in which they were abused and/or witnessed abuse. The only way to break the cycle of abuse is to get professional help. You cannot love him out of this. You will never be good enough to get him to stop abusing you. He needs help. Staying will only enable his behavior.

Why you may have attracted this:

- Were your own parents physically abusive to you? Was the only time they paid attention to you when they were hitting you? We learn as children that bad attention is better than no attention.

- Is physical abuse the way that you learned to experience love from a young age? If so you may actually not just attract physical abusers, but verbal abusers as well.

- Did you take on the belief from your childhood that you are deserving of abuse, or that abuse equals love? Remember everything that happens before the age of 14, we experience in the mind of a child, and if you were abused early on, you will probably believe that in some way you deserved it. Get professional help for this. These are beliefs that you can change.

He is verbally abusive to you.

Verbal abuse is not as obvious as physical abuse because the scars are all internal. But make no mistake verbal abuse can be just as damaging as physical abuse and erodes your sense of self-worth just the same. And if you ever marry a verbal abuser, rest assured it will ONLY get worse if he doesn't get some professional help. Once people are married, the very worst of their behavior comes up because they are under the assumption that the other person can't run. Just like physical abusers, verbal abusers don't change unless they get professional help of some kind. You will never be good enough to get him to stop so don't even bother trying.

Verbal abuse includes being called names by your partner, being yelled at or screamed at, being cursed at, being threatened or being blamed for your partner's abusive behavior. Some verbal abusers disguise their words as constructive criticism so just know that if it feels like a put down, it probably is (*http://divorcesupport.about.com*).

Why is he doing this? He's scared, that's why. A Course in Miracles says that all attack is a cry for help. He may be afraid that you will leave him (as perhaps a parent did in the past) so he verbally beats you down so that you think you are so awful that no one else will want you. Perhaps he saw his father verbally abuse his mother as a way of keeping her and this is the only way he knows to behave in a relationship. Know that the things he says about you are about him, not you. If he calls you mean and irresponsible, it's more than likely he is the one that is mean and irresponsible. If he calls you a whore, he's probably the one out cruising for other women to have sex with. If he calls you a gold-digger, it's probably because he's insecure about his ability to provide. (You can speak to a trusted friend or counselor about if there is any shred of truth in these awful accusations. But I believe that feedback that is worthy of being listened to and internalized is always delivered with love and not attack.)

Why you may have attracted this:

- Does he speak to you the way your mother or father (or other adult figures) spoke to you when you were young (or still speak to you now)? If so, you must heal your issues with your critical parent so that you don't keep attracting your mother or father as a partner. In fact, it would be greatly helpful to work with a therapist or coach to learn to set boundaries with the people in your life as in, "you may not speak to me this way. If you continue to do so, I will leave and you will not have me in your life." And if you say it, you need to follow through. This man is giving you a grand opportunity for growth here, the opportunity to stand up for yourself.

He's a "swooper."

You know the type – the guy who comes on strong at the beginning and then disappears. And then "swoops" back in with all of his romantic talk and promises, and then does not deliver; only to wait months later and do the same thing over, and over, again. This guy preys on the fact that women are suckers for love and he will play the role of the Knight in Shining Armor until it's not fun anymore. Or maybe he delivers on some promises and is sweet *some* of the time, but the neglectful crap you have to put up with most of the time is really ridiculous.

I also like to call these guys "Mr. Variable Reinforcement" after the behavior psychology studies done by B.F. Skinner. The basic gist of the study is that Skinner had a bunch of rats. The rats learned that when they pressed a bar in their cage they got a food pellet. Skinner experimented with different schedules of reward, one being a fixed schedule and the other being a variable schedule. On the fixed schedule, a rat got a pellet after every 3 presses of the bar (or 5 or 20 presses but it was a consistent number in each trial). The rat would learn how many times it had to press the bar to get the goodie and wouldn't bother with pressing it at other times. In the variable schedule, a rat would have to press the bar 3 times, then 20, then 1, then 15, etc. to get the goodie. The reward schedule was variable. Because the rats couldn't figure out the exact interval for getting the goodie, they kept pressing the bar hoping that this time would be the one that they got it. Skinner concluded that the variable reward schedule produces both the highest rate of responding and the greatest resistance to extinction of the behavior. (This theory explains why people like slot machines) *(http://users.ipfw.edu/abbott/120/Schedules.html)*.

OK ladies do you see what I'm getting at here? For all of you wondering why you just can't get over that jerk (who is nice to you on a variable schedule), Mr. B.F.

Skinner just laid it out. We are the rats wondering when we're going to get a goodie (love, attention, validation, sex, etc.). You keep pressing that bar (giving him chances, being good to him, giving him your time and energy and your body) and when he finally does something nice to reciprocate you think, "Yay. I won!" (Only you really didn't win because you have to keep going through this awful nonsense.) Variable Reinforcement may be exciting in gambling, but it's a pretty miserable way to exist in a relationship if you haven't noticed.

Why you may have attracted this:

- Well let me ask you this: was your father Mr. Variable Reinforcement? For most of your childhood was he checked out, drunk or high, absent, or even abusive, with variably placed memories of him being truly present or loving? If that was the case then it's no wonder that this scenario would seem familiar and comfortable in your intimate relationships. And please don't think you're alone in this experience. I would venture to say in our culture this is more the rule than the exception. And if this is the case, don't despair because you are not permanently ruined from having a loving relationship. The first step to healing is identifying the pattern.

- What's interesting is that I've met women who had loving and present fathers who still fall for Mr. Variable Reinforcement. What's up with that? Well, I can only offer my personal opinion. I think these women (and many other people on Earth quite frankly) believe in a variably available God or have a variable experience of spirituality. Do you believe that we live in a harsh and unloving world punctuated by a few brief, fleeting and random moments of connectedness and meaning? This belief will certainly be reflected in your relationships. You may find yourself becoming attached to Mr. Random Reinforcement and his random and infrequent "goodies" because what else can you expect in a random, unloving Universe devoid of sensible order?

He doesn't fight fair.

Fair fighting means making room for the viewpoints of both partners. A man who totally invalidates your opinions and views is a control-freak. If he cannot recognize and be willing to work on this, it is definitely a red flag.

Fighting fair involves keeping your fights private (possibly with the exception of a close friend or relative and/or a therapist depending on what is comfortable for both of you). Fights should not be aired publically in front of others or on Facebook. Everyone should not know your business nor should someone else confront you about what is wrong in your relationship. Part of maintaining the sanctity of a relationship is keeping the inner workings private between the two people involved.

Fair fighting does not involve character assassination, intimidation or bullying. A man who calls you names or attacks you personally is hitting below the belt. He has every right to express when he does not agree with or is bothered by your behavior, but flipping out and attacking your character instead of the issue is not acceptable.

A man who is centered in stability and love will let you retreat from a fight with your dignity intact and not need to knock you down or have you grovel for his forgiveness. If you are wrong or wish you had acted differently, acknowledge that and apologize. A mature man will give you the space to correct yourself without having to demolish your sense of self or putting you beneath him *(www.drphil.com)*.

This does not mean that the fact that you fight is in and of itself a red flag. Carolyn Cowan, a longtime marriage and family researcher at the University of California, Berkeley, said that, "We need to learn to tolerate conflict in our relationships." In a study in which "University of Washington researchers studied newlywed couples and learned, not surprisingly, that those who rarely argued were happier in their relationship than those who fought often. But three years later, the findings had reversed. Couples with an early history of bickering had worked out their problems and were more likely to be in stable marriages. The couples who'd avoided conflict early on were more likely to be in troubled relationships or already divorced" *(http://www.oprah.com/relationships/Relationship-Red-Flags-and-the-Science-Behind-a-Good-Marriage)*. Fighting in a relationship is natural and normal, as feelings regularly need to be aired. A red flag is only present when there is a spirit of meanness, vicious attack or degradation behind the fighting.

Why you may have attracted this:

- Do you fight fair?
- Do you validate his viewpoints and give him the space to express himself to you?
- Is your need to be right greater than your need to have peace?
- Have you asked yourself, "What parts of this conflict are coming from me?" and really reflected on your role in the fighting.
- Are you proficient at discussing your feelings in a non-hysterical, non-reactive manner?
- Did you learn as a child that the only way to get your emotional needs met (get attention) was to act out against your parental figure, probably a father? If so you will effectively teach your partner to treat you with disrespect.
- As a child did your father repeatedly invalidate you and is it possible you've projected that pattern onto your partner?
- Do you feel like a victim? If so, you will attract an intimidator.

The tough part about differing opinions in a relationship is the following: according to Dr. Pat Allen, a man's highest psychic need is to have his thoughts respected. A woman's highest psychic need is to have her feelings cherished. For a relationship to work, you can't have it both ways. You either get to choose the masculine or the feminine role and if you choose the masculine then you put him in the feminine. This is not a role that most men want to be in and they will either continue to fight for their position to points of utter frustration or they will leave. What that means is that for him to be the man in the relationship, you must respect his opinions and thoughts and put them first, especially if you want him to cherish your feelings and put them first. You may express your disagreement or that his choices do not make you comfortable and it will be up to him to make a new choice that will suit you both because he cherishes your feelings and puts them first. This is the subtle distinction of how equality and balance is achieved in a relationship. He leads but you have ultimate veto power. And ladies, the easiest way for this to work is to make sure that you choose to be with a man who's thoughts and opinions you actually do respect. (Allen 42-56)

He likes disturbing pornography.

This is an interesting subject because obviously what each person finds disturbing is totally different, so I'm just going to discuss a few things I've learned along the way.

First, listen to your instincts. If something strikes YOU as disturbing or not quite right about a man's pornography preferences, confront him and/or run.

Second, men like to look at porn. We know this. Men are visual creatures and are turned on by watching sex. Again, this is completely normal.

However, *addictively* watching pornography is not normal. Porn addiction is defined by Wikipedia as a "dependence upon pornography characterized by obsessive viewing, reading, and thinking about pornography and sexual themes to the **detriment of**

other areas of life." Pornography can be used like alcohol, drugs or food as a form of escapism. I don't know anyone who doesn't participate in some form of escapism so shaming a man for his use of pornography in that regard is not helpful. Again, the problem and red flag lies in whether his viewing of porn negatively affects other aspects of his life. Is he late to work meetings because of porn? Is he unable to engage in loving sexual acts with you in the absence of pornographic stimulation? Does he look at porn in places where it is totally inappropriate like at work or on line at the supermarket?

There are a few bottom lines here. Again, I defer to Dan Savage who does not consider anything involving children, animals or excrement to be within the realm of being "GGG" (which is why most of that stuff is illegal) and I think this goes for pornography as well. A man who is aroused by pornography involving children or animals (both of whom are incapable of consent) or excrement, is dealing with MAJOR issues. This is a humongous, blaring red flag. Don't rationalize this or allow him to. Run immediately. And run fast.

Beyond that, there are a few distinctions to make. A man that likes gay porn, man on man, is most likely gay or bisexual. Straight men do not get off on gay porn. Period.

A study done by Meredith Shivers in 2006 proves this point: A variety of sexual videos were shown to men and women, gay and straight. The videos included the following configurations: man/woman, man/man, woman/woman, lone man masturbating, lone woman masturbating, a muscular guy walking naked on a beach, a fit woman working out in the nude and a short film of bonobos mating. The test subjects had a keypad where they recorded how turned on they were by each film and devices hooked up to their genitals to measure blood flow as an indicator that they were getting turned on.

What she found was that "gay or straight, the men were predictable. The things that turned them on were what you'd expect. The straight guys responded to anything involving naked women, but were left cold when only men were on display." The gay guys responded to anything involving naked men or men having sex but were disinterested in anything else. The measure of genital blood flow coincided with the subjective rating of how much they were turned on in both gay and straight men. Or as authors Christopher Ryan and Cacilda Jetha quipped, "As it turns out, men can think with both heads at once, as long as both are thinking the same thing" (Ryan and Jetha 272-273).

A man that likes to watch porn where a man is being "pegged" by a woman (a woman penetrates a man's anus with a strap on dildo) or "rimmed" (oral-anal sex) by a woman is straight. It doesn't matter what activities are being performed, as long as they are being performed by a woman to a man, the man who likes to watch them is straight. Again, if your man is watching porn involving these activities, you can assume that he would like to experience them in real life and whether or not you find these activities objectionable is totally to your discretion.

As for pornography involving gangbangs (many men on one woman), authors Ryan and Jetha indicate a preference to view this is not as weird and depraved as one might think (231-232). In fact, they systematically present several arguments to indicate that polyamorous sexual practices are our sexual anthropological roots prior to its condemnation by modern-day religions. In tribal cultures, many men would have sex with one woman, presumably when she was ovulating and therefore in an amorous mood, and their sperm would compete to ensure that the strongest offspring from the most compatible genetics would be produced. They argue that women are generally louder during sex as a mating call to bring around men who want to participate with her, which is why women moaning and screaming is still such a turn-on to men today (253-258). They also provide evidence to our polyamorous roots from indigenous tribes, untouched by Western religious practices, which still partake in group-sex as a natural and normal expression of sexuality. For example, in some tribes of the Amazon, they believe that it is possible for a child to have many fathers and already pregnant women are encouraged to have sex with the most able hunters, the best story-tellers, the smartest healers, so that their unborn child could get some of these qualities (91).

Men who enjoy watching porn in which many men have sex with one woman may simply be responding to evolutionary imperatives. Men who like to watch their wives have sex with other, possibly more virile men, would not be considered depraved 3000 years ago because the result of that sort of behavior would be stronger tribes. Whether actually having multiple partners in real life is appropriate in your relationship is up to you and your partner, but his viewing of polyamorous sex is not necessarily a red flag.

The thing about porn is that when men view it they can get off and don't have to risk rejection. It's seldom about watching "perfect"-looking, sexually experienced women. As women that's generally what we think it's about, but according to research interviews done by Brene Brown, it is not. When Brown spoke with a male therapist who has done extensive work with men, he said, "from the time boys are eight to ten years old, they learn that initiating sex is their responsibility and that sexual rejection soon becomes the hallmark of masculine shame...I guess the secret is that sex is terrifying for most men. That's why you see everything from porn to the violent, desperate attempts to exercise power and control. Rejection is deeply painful" [Brown 103].

Ladies, can we begin to understand this? If there is a man in your life, just know that the power of making him feel worthy or shamed lies in part in your hands. We tend to think that we are the only ones who are vulnerable around issues of sexuality but that is false. The man you are engaging with has to be just as vulnerable, if not more. When a man feels sexually rejected, there's a chance he will turn to porn to numb the pain. Now that does not mean that we can't exert our wants, needs, preferences and/or turn down sex when it is not right for us. But it changed everything for me to know how sensitive men can be about sex and to make sure that my communication in that area is clear and kind.

I don't ever recommend spying on a man to snoop and see what sorts of pornography he has on his computer or in his possession. I don't believe that we need to resort to that type of behavior when the truth always presents itself in time. But I do wholeheartedly encourage discussing what sorts of erotica you and your partner like and dislike.

Why you may have attracted this:

I don't think there are universal reasons for attracting this type, although I do think that this is a red flag to be discussed.

He hates weddings.

Now he doesn't have to LOVE weddings the way most women do, but a man who hates weddings will most likely not be walking down the aisle anytime soon. This can be in the form of a severe distaste for attending weddings, sneering during weddings about how the groom is about to "bite the dust" or be imprisoned by his new life of matrimonial hell, or a refusal to go to your family or friends' weddings with you. A man for whom commitment and marriage are abhorrent will most likely not be able to be vulnerable with you or move forward with you in life.

*This happened to me.** I was dating a guy for a few months when I got invited to a friend's wedding out of town. I asked him if he'd like to go with me thinking that it would be so much fun. When he said "no" and that he hated weddings, I couldn't believe it. How could someone hate weddings? I couldn't believe that he would prefer that I go to a wedding by myself and have all of the guys there hitting on me because I was there alone. I did end up going to that wedding alone and I should have broken up with the guy right then and there. He never was as serious about me as I was about him and the signs were right there when he refused to come to that wedding with me because he hated weddings. A man who was serious about me would have jumped on the opportunity to be by my side for one of my friend's most important days.

Why you may have attracted this:

- How do you feel about marriage? Do you feel it's a trap? Search yourself honestly here.

- Do you believe you are worthy of committing to?

- Do you believe there are honest, loving men out there who will commit to you or do you believe that all men are dogs so you might as well hold onto the one you've got even though he doesn't cherish you or make you feel particularly special?

He's told you that he's not able to be faithful and/or has cheated on all his girlfriends in the past.

Monogamy is not for everyone. Most of us don't like to hear this and believe that everyone should be able to sexually restrain themselves to one person for the rest of their lives, but this is simply not true. Some men want monogamy and some don't. (If you are a person who believes in open relationships and wants to partake in one, this may actually not be a red flag for you). Ask a man what he thinks about marriage and monogamy. As long as you maintain an open and accepting demeanor, he will probably tell you the truth. A man that says he doesn't know how he will feel about monogamy, has cheated on girlfriends in the past, or openly admits to wanting to sleep with or date lots of women is telling the truth. (Try to be as unattached as possible when you ask this. Men who sense that you're going to flip out if you don't like their answer will lie.)

You are a great woman, but for a man who is not interested in monogamy, you will never be good enough for him to decide he will only want to sleep with you. It has nothing to do with you. Maybe one day he will get sick of giving his emotional and sexual attention to more than one woman and will want monogamy. Do you want to wait around for that day?

"Serial male cheaters are usually driven by a combination of higher testosterone levels and early childhood experiences, which affect how relationships are perceived as adults" (Pease 128). So while it's probably not practical to give him a hormone test, it is reasonable to ask a man within the first few dates what he thinks about relationships, how he experienced his parents' relationship (either with each other or the other partners they had) and what kind of relationship he wants for himself. I don't believe that a man should automatically be condemned because his father was a philanderer. As a child, he had no control over these circumstances. But having that type of father as a childhood role model can have a powerful influence on a man and it is up to you to talk to him to see where he stands with regard to those influences.

Why you may have attracted this:

- How do you feel about monogamy? You attract what you are and if you are confused about your desire to only have sexual relations with one person, you will attract a similar person. This is hard because much of society tells us that monogamy is the only right way to do a relationship and shames women more than men on this issue. The fact is that the only right way to do a relationship is the way the two people in it have agreed to do it. Keeping agreements is a much more useful measure of integrity than not having sexual desires for another person.

- Do you believe that you are worthy of being committed to? If not, your man won't either.

- Do you believe that men can be monogamous? You will attract a man based on your beliefs so if you don't believe it's possible then men who are non-monogamous will show up to prove you right.

He's not there for you in a crisis. (An even earlier red flag is he doesn't put your feelings first).

You are always there for him to help with what he needs and then your mother gets cancer or your father has a stroke and he disappears. Or you ask him to escort you to your mother's funeral and he whines. This man is a selfish little boy. If he cannot be there for you in these times of major crisis, he will not be able to be there for you for all of the crazy things that occur in a marriage. Do you want to go through life essentially alone while legally bound to someone else? Consider it a blessing that you know what you're dealing with before you're married to this man. I can't tell you how many women have said to me, "I should have broken up with him long before I did. In fact, I should've broken up with him when [insert crisis-death of a family member or major illness] and he wasn't able to be there for me."

Why you may have attracted this:

- Do you know how to communicate your feelings honestly and calmly, without hysteria? If you are always hysterical, your partner may not be able to register a *true* crisis.

- Do you believe that you are allowed to have feelings, be vulnerable and be the cared for party in the relationship?

- Are you able to receive help or do you run around constantly giving help to others?

- Have you created a culture in your relationship where you always put his needs first, ignoring your own?

- Have you pretended to be a low-maintenance girl so that he would stay and not leave because you are too much work? Is this man now treating you like the woman you have pretended to be? A healthy woman puts herself first always and realizes that she cannot give to her man unless she has given to herself first (Allen 59). A mature man put his woman's feelings first and feels masculine while comforting her in times of need. He may not know how to share his own feelings or say all the right things, but he will most certainly know how to hold you, how to listen and how to just be there. But it is your job to learn to become vulnerable with a man. A woman's vulnerability sometimes miraculously causes a man to realize his masculine protective nature. But if it doesn't, consider this an early warning sign and act accordingly.

- Did you mother essentially do the job of both your mother and father either because she was a single mother or because your father was totally checked out? If so you may be unconsciously repeating this pattern or choosing a man who is a little boy to show loyalty to your mother and her struggle. The truth is your mother would (or should) be happy and proud to see you find a man who is grounded in his masculine strength to give you support when you need it.

- Do you believe that men are incapable little boys, perhaps because your father acted like one?

You've been dating 6 months and you haven't met his parents or anyone close to him. (Or he is resistant to meeting your family.)

A man who is serious about you will want to introduce you to the people that are important to him. He will keep you a secret if he is not. (Likewise, a man who puts up any resistance to meeting your family is probably doing so because he knows his intentions with you are not what your family would like to hear. He has reservations about being with you and feels that once he meets your family he will be cornered into a commitment. A man who is serious about you will meet your family with confidence and pride.)

Now it may be that he feels embarrassed by his family. If this is the case, I'm sure he still has friends, colleagues or surrogate family that is important to him.

If you haven't met them, I would start to wonder why and consider more closely what is really going on in your relationship.

Why you may have attracted this:

- Are you embarrassed to introduce him to your family?

- Do you believe you are worthy of being an important part of a man's life?

- Do you believe that any man would be lucky to have you and should feel privileged to introduce you to his family? If the answer if no, you have attracted the fact that you should remain a secret.

- Have you had "the talk" with your man and do you know where you stand with him? If it's been six months and you haven't met anyone close to him it's possible that he may think that you are in a casual relationship. It's time to talk to him about it and find out where he stands. Yes, the answer may hurt if it's not what you want to hear but it's better to know the truth.

- Are you a judgmental person? If his family is dysfunctional or embarrassing, the last thing he needs to hear is your verbal or energetic confirmation of that fact and he will probably delay or avoid your meeting. Are you able to meet people who may be different from you with an open mind?

He wants you to change.

I understand that it's normal for men to want to "fix" things. Men are generally solution-oriented and enterprising in their view of the world. He may think you are great and see even greater potential in you and that is wonderful (Allen 71). In a relationship, we are supposed to see our partner's highest potential.

But when you are not acceptable as you are it's a red flag. Beware of the man that wants you to lose weight, change your hair color or get plastic surgery as a way to please him. This man does not love you. He loves what he wants to make you. Do you want to live the rest of your life like this, walking on eggshells to be acceptable to this man? This type of man will probably hold you down and make you think you are not good enough to keep your self-esteem low so that you think you need him and will never leave him. If he wants someone thinner, blonder, bigger busted, tanner, fitter, more educated, more religious or quieter, he should go find her and leave you alone. A man who tells you what to do and how you should behave is acting like your father. His fatherly behavior will ultimately turn you off so that you don't want to have sex with him anymore and then you've got big problems in the relationship.

Why you may have attracted this:

- Was your own father disapproving and invalidating of you? Or did you not have a father and now you've attracted this man to be your father figure? Romantic interests are inappropriate as father figures. It is more important to heal your relationship with your own father.

- A great question I learned from my own therapist,

John McMullin, is "can you allow this man to own his judgments of you so that you no longer have to own them"? When you fight against someone's judgment of you, you drive it deeper into your energy. But when you stay unattached to what others think of you, you do not accept their poison in the form of judgments.

- Do you believe that you are good enough? If not, you will continue to attract men who validate this belief.

- Do you believe God loves you exactly as you are and that He knew exactly what he was doing when he made you?

- Do you believe you are deserving of love exactly as you are? Do you believe that it's possible for someone to love you exactly as you are? Again, there are women out there who some would judge as unattractive, fat, uneducated, plain, out of shape, too skinny, unsexy or boring and some of them are happily married with men who love them exactly as they are because they believe that they deserve to be loved.

He's homophobic.

How many anti-gay politicians do we need to catch with gay prostitutes before it's obvious that most people who hate gays are closet-gays? Beware of anyone who protests that much about homosexuality. Such a negative charge on a preference that is accepted today as normal is a red flag. It's a bad sign when a man cannot have compassion for the most disenfranchised people in our society. I'm not saying he has to march in the Gay Pride Parade, but a man who harbors hatred and cannot "live and let live," is a ticking time bomb of anger. This anger will surely be released into your life in some way. If this man is going to teach values to your children, do you want them to learn prejudice and hatred? A man who is comfortable with his own sexuality will allow others to have their own sexual preferences. Yes everyone is entitled to their own values around the subject of sexuality, the key here is that active verbal aggression or worse against gay people is a red flag that you are dealing with an angry, judgmental person and that will surely manifest in other places in your relationship.

I've been on dates with homophobic men. And the truth is that I lose all respect for them once I hear any disparaging comments about gay people in general. There is nowhere to go with a man if I have no respect for him. Real men who are grounded in security and self-confidence will use their power to protect the weaker members of society instead of speaking out against them.

Why you may have attracted this:

- I don't think there are universal reasons for attracting this type, although I do think that this is a red flag to be discussed.

He lies, even about little things.

Lying is an absolute bottom line. You cannot build a

life with someone who frequently lies or leaves out important truths. This will come back to bite you in the butt at some point.

Shakespeare said, "the truth shall set you free" and he was right. Even truly awful past deeds can be forgiven, learned from and healed when they are brought to the light of truth. No matter what this man has done in the past, he must be able to be honest with you about it or you will both be living a lie.

That means you must listen to him and do your best to remain calm, compassionate, non-hysterical and non-judgmental when he does tell you his truth. If you listen with your whole body to get a sense of the place he is coming from now, you will know if he has moved past these painful events and is trying to live a more honest and conscientious life.

Even lying about little things (saying he went to the movies when he really went to the strip club) can be indicative of a bigger problem: he's not comfortable with his needs and who he is, he doesn't feel he can trust you or women in general, he enjoys having parts of his life that are secretive and scandalous. These can all be problems down the line when there is more at stake. Relatively benign lies can lead to big ones later on and are indicative that there is a problem.

If you see him lie to other people, especially family and friends, he is probably lying to you. If this is the way he moves through life, don't believe that you are special or immune to it. A liar is a liar until they really decide to change. It is said that the way a person does one thing, is the way he does everything.

I would sooner trust an ex-convict who was totally

honest about his past and committed to change than a wealthy businessman that I've caught in several lies and feels no remorse or accountability for his lying.

Why you may have attracted this:

- Are you a liar? Are there parts of your life that you are not living in total integrity? If so, the liars you've attracted are holding up a mirror to you to take a look at your own behavior.

- Do you desperately need a rescuer? Are you so desperate for security, for "everything to be OK" and a knight in shining armor, that you will turn a blind eye to clear signs that everything is not OK?

- Do you desperately need a father? Women who had absentee fathers may still be pining for a man whom they can wholeheartedly trust to take care of them, even if certain things he's said don't check out. No man can be your father and he will ultimately let you down because in an adult relationship this is not his role. Consider why you may feel unable to create your own emotional, spiritual or financial security.

BEYOND THE 2 YEAR MARK

When the hormone surge has died

Researchers have proven that after 2 years the love hormones that flooded couples' brains at the beginning of a relationship have returned to normal levels. Yet many couples remain together after two years and report that they are still happy and just as excited about their partner as they were in the beginning which means that there is much more than hormones involved in the longevity of a relationship. Mother Nature does her best to create a love cocktail in the brain to bring us together (and hopefully to get us to procreate) for the first two years, but the rest is up to us. There is no real accepted predictor of what keeps couples happily together in the long run. Even with all of the studies and theories we have, love and relationships are still pretty much a crapshoot (Pease 28-29).

After 2 years of being with someone, there aren't too many red flags. You really know that person inside and out. However, if you suspect that your partner is having an affair, there are behavioral changes that could prove that you are correct. According to authors Allan and Barbara Pease, here are the eight signs that you may be dealing with a cheater:

Routine changes- "any change in behaviors that have been part of your life as a couple can indicate a driving force outside the home: A man starts doing his own washing; an armchair TV addict joins a gym; your partner stops wearing a wedding ring or starts locking drawers..."

Sex changes- this could be that your partner is suddenly disinterested in sex. Or out of the blue, they want to try new things they have never asked about before.

Appearance changes- "dieting, new clothes, showers the minute they walk in the door, him shaving twice a day"

Business trips- "increased trips away, more than the usual number of overnighters, failure to invite you to business events, secrecy or vagueness about schedules, failure to share flight or hotel information, not being where one is supposed to be. Alternatively, he might start working late into the evening, or you may notice that [his] workmates are uncomfortable around you."

Nervous reactions- "when the phone rings or when you mention a certain person at his work. Also look out for talking in [his] sleep, erratic mood swings, and increased criticism of you."

Conversation changes- when he starts talking about a certain woman more than usual there is likely something going on. Or perhaps he stops talking about a certain woman all together. A man who repeats stories multiple times is also an indicator because he can't remember to whom he told what.

Technology changes- "you start to notice that your partner prefers to email you rather than call you. When he calls you, conversations are kept short, end abruptly or are whispered, all signs that someone else may be present. [He] has constant excuses to go for a walk with [his] mobile phone...or [he] goes to the toilet too often and for too long. When you are together, he doesn't want to pick up certain incoming calls in your presence. [He] is constantly online, even when with you, checking e-mails, and if you approach, the window on the computer is closed suddenly. His BlackBerry is never left lying around where you might see it. [His} computer and phone suddenly have passwords."

New friends- he has friends that you never get to meet. When they call, he keeps the conversations very brief. Or maybe you find out that some of his new friends are cheaters. This is a major red flag that he is one as well (Pease 135-136).

NOW THAT YOU HAVE IDENTIFIED THE PATTERNS, WHAT DO YOU DO?

1) Work on yourself via psychological counseling, coaching, self-help books or seminars and 2) pray. Those are the only answers and the surest way out. And they work best when performed in concert with each other. Psychological counseling without increased spiritual awareness lacks the power to make a big enough change in your life. You may understand what your pathology is, how it happened and dissect every word your mother and father ever said to you, but it is the Higher Power that creates the powerful miracle of a change in perception that helps lift us out. Likewise, you can pray to a Higher Power to heal you all you want, but without the specific feedback of a therapist or coach, we often lack the psychological skills to create new patterns of behavior.

The first 3 steps of any 12 Step program are:

1. We admitted we were powerless over alcohol (or in this case: dysfunctional relationships, low self-worth, feelings of loneliness, inability to attract a healthy relationship or whatever pattern you feel is plaguing you) — that our lives had become unmanageable.

2. Came to believe that a Power greater than ourselves could restore us to sanity.

3. Made a decision to turn our will and our lives over to the care of God, as we understood Him.

We admit that we have a problem that we are powerless to change. There is a place in our psyche where we have falsely learned that love should be painful, abusive or neglectful. We have been taught by adults who didn't know better that we are not deserving of an abundance of love exactly as we are. So, we pray to God to intervene and help us release our negative patterns and attachments. Acknowledging the patterns on a cognitive level is not enough. The quickest way to heal is to appeal to the loving Spirit within and around us.

Each relationship we go through has immense potential for learning. Say to God, "I give this relationship to You to use for Your purposes. Thank You for guiding me." And God will use your relationship to heal you but maybe not in the way you think. If you pray to God to heal your feelings of worthlessness, He may not necessarily send you a partner who says how wonderful you are all the time. He may send you someone who treats you less than worthily so you can decide within yourself that you are worth more than this and leave the relationship to find one that is more in line with your new sense of self-worth. Or if you ask God to heal your inclinations toward entanglements with married men, God may actually send you another married man so that you can make the conscious choice to walk away before you get emotionally involved, thereby creating a new pattern of behavior and sense of deserving an available partner. Once you have sufficiently learned this lesson, God will no longer need to send it you anymore.

"'Dear God, I surrender this relationship to you,' means, 'Dear God, let me see this person through your eyes.'…we are asking to see as God sees, think as God thinks, love as God loves. We are asking for help in seeing someone's innocence" (Williamson 94).

I was once having a familiar trouble in a relationship. I had a pattern of men getting close to me and then forcefully pushing me away. And it happened again. And I was at home crying and in a lot of pain. I was in so much emotional pain that I actually made myself sick. I made the conscious choice in that moment to give the relationship to God. And wouldn't you know two days later the guy called me in the middle of the night telling me exactly why he pushed me away; that he was still obsessed with two of his ex-girlfriends and was dealing with all sorts of anxiety and depression around it. He told me that he came from an extremely abusive family and felt like he was cracking up. He decided that he needed therapy and that getting involved with me wouldn't be healthy for either of us. His confession made me have compassion for the inner struggle he was going through. And it made it easier for me to let go. I forgave him.

Forgiveness is major, for what you don't forgive will continue to remain in your energy field. I like the saying, "resentment is like swallowing a pill of poison and expecting the other person to die." Holding on to past grievances harms you, not the "offender." Pray to be able to forgive and release this person (or pray to forgive and release the initial "offender" maybe a parent whose actions you've projected onto your romantic partner). As it says in A Course in Miracles, "Every situation, properly perceived, becomes an opportunity to heal." Ask God to heal your perceptions. If you do so, God will help show you the pain that is causing the other person to act the way they do. And when this happens you too will experience the maturity of true compassion that sets you free. In this way, we transform red flags into markers of humanity that allow us to have empathy for our fellow humans. This does not necessarily mean it is appropriate to continue in an intimate relationship with this person, but the relationship will have become holy because you have used the conflict to heal one or both parties.

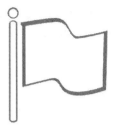

WHITE FLAGS

A white flag is a sign that it is time for you to surrender (break up with him and get help immediately). You are literally so beat down physically, mentally, emotionally or spiritually that you feel like you want to wave the white flag of surrender. Sadly, many women think they are supposed to suffer for love and have lost touch with what a personal violation actually feels like. Here are some examples of white flags.

You need to go on medication to stay in the relationship.

Like anti-anxiety meds or anti-depressants (or even illegal drugs!).

You should not need to go on medication to stay in any relationship, even a marriage. Go to a qualified therapist and get help. If your relationship is the only factor causing you to ask your doctor for mood elevators, you have a problem. This is your intuition screaming at you to either get out (especially if you are not married) or make major change within the relationship like going for joint counseling (especially if you are married). There's a tongue in cheek saying, "Before you diagnose yourself with depression or low self-esteem, first make sure you are not, in fact, surrounded by assholes." There is some real validity to that saying.

His behavior is erratic and/or he is driving you crazy.

The man who loves you and is going to be there for you is very much invested in your sanity. Only a needy, sick person will thrive on your insanity. He may need professional help and if he will not get it alone or with you, you're in for some troubling times. You don't want to live this way, walking on eggshells for the rest of your life. Throw in the towel, get help and regain the peace that God intends for us.

Your behavior is so disgusting, evil or pathetic that you can't look at yourself in the mirror anymore.

This is not who you are. You are a beautiful, loving person. A relationship is supposed to serve God, the Higher Purpose in Life, the Purposes of Love, Growth, Understanding and Joy. It should not make both people utter lunatics that hurt each other viciously. This is when you need to step back and reassess. What is going on here? Get an outside opinion from a TRUSTED source. Pray for help and throw up the white flag in surrender and get a grip before you decide on your next move.

You have gotten into a routine of doing things with him sexually that make you uncomfortable and you don't know how to say no.

Many women have fallen into this destructive pattern, which erodes one's self-esteem from the inside. First, have you communicated to him that said acts make you uncomfortable? This may be enough to solve the problem. If it is not, get help so that you are no longer a silent observer of your own exploitation.

Your friends hate him. All of them.

If all of your friends (family, colleagues, clients) can't

stand to hear you talk about a man anymore, it's because his behavior is disrespectful or abusive and you need to get out. You can rationalize it if one or two of your friends don't like him or your relationship, because maybe they are jealous or judgmental. But if ALL of your friends don't like him, run. This is bad news. If they end up doing an intervention with you over this guy, wave the white flag.

He forces you to get an abortion against your will. You've had more than one abortion by this man.

Any man who has the disrespect to get you pregnant and then forces you to have an abortion is selfish in the worst way. This entire cycle of events is extremely traumatic on a woman and you must get out and get help. The residual emotional trauma of an event like this can have far reaching effects so please don't go through this alone. Seek the help of a private therapist or go to *www.plannedparenthood.org* for counseling and support.

You clean his room, find him jobs, make sure he does his homework, make sure his bills are paid, make sure he keeps his appointments, pack his suitcase, do his laundry, etc.

Girl what are you doing? You are acting like his mother and, frankly, no man wants to have sex with his mother. You are killing the eroticism in the

124

relationship. If you have already gotten to this place in the relationship, you need to take a major step back. (I'm not talking about once you're in a marriage or domestic partnership and there is an agreed upon division of labor to keep the family running well, that's different. I'm talking about creating a pattern at the beginning of a relationship in which you are micromanaging him. This is so damaging.)

Some women say, well if I don't do these things for him they won't get done. He'll be a slob, go into debt, not find work, not have clean clothes, forget things for our vacation, etc. And that is precisely the point. A man who cannot take care of his basic needs is not a man but a boy and one day you will majorly resent the fact that you have become his mother. When you have 2 screaming kids and a filthy house and you need some real help, do you think this man is going to be the one to give it to you? Not only that, but when he finally breaks up with you because your help makes him realize exactly how pathetic he is, you are going to be so angry and resentful feeling that you put all of this work into a non-receptive person. Save your energy, work on yourself and find a grown-up man.

A healthy woman takes care of herself first and foremost because she knows that if she doesn't she will have nothing to give to those in her life anyway.

Are you afraid to find a real man because you believe that this little boy NEEDS you, which means he will never leave you? This is not true. Only a real man centered in his own self-confidence can give you any kind of real love anyway.

EPILOGUE

"Everything will be okay in the end. If it's not okay, it's not the end." –Unknown (and frequently seen on Facebook.)

"It is your birthright to discover your sacred contract. It will guide you to find your divine destiny." -Caroline Myss

Believe it or not, there is a happy ending to all of this.

I know, how can I say that? At the time of this writing, I'm 35 years old, I've gone through all of these red flags in dating and I'm still single. Still out there, still plugging away and looking for the one. I have not met my happy ending yet. So why am I still optimistic?

An idea I got from A Course in Miracles is the belief that God has an individual life curriculum for each of us. God puts people and situations in our lives to create the perfect classroom for that curriculum and to bring about the lessons we are to learn. And how do we navigate the classroom? By listening to our intuition, by forgiving those whom we feel have done us wrong and by following our joy. I believe that our soul mate is perfectly placed along the way and he will present himself at the perfect time when we are ready to receive him. My path is different than yours so I cannot tell you what the path is to meet your soul mate. However, I know in my heart and I have seen from examples of others around me that when you listen to the deepest callings of your Heart and Soul, it is inevitable that you must meet your soul mate. It could take minutes or it could take years. But right now consider the following two questions:

1) Is there something that you feel that you are being called to do that you are not doing?

2) What do you think is blocking you from finding and receiving love?

I'll bet that you have an answer to both questions. (Hint: whatever came to your mind when you just read them is the answer!)

When you sit and get quiet with yourself and reflect, in meditation, journaling, exercise or whatever activity or non-activity gets you to clear your mind, you know the answers. If you don't know the answers, take a moment to ask the Universe for guidance and I guarantee you WILL know the answers.

I asked myself these two questions a little while back and I actually verbalized the answers to some family members. I knew that my biggest block to love was not feeling like I had myself together financially. Being in debt was wrecking my self-esteem. My family told me I was crazy and that lots of women met their husbands when they were in debt, which I know is true. However, I know that it is true for me that I will not meet my husband until I feel like I really have myself together financially. I don't know why it's true – I just know that it is.

And as for the thing that I feel that I'm being called to do: well it's to write, specifically to write about my experiences in relationships. As I mentioned at the beginning, I am not a therapist by trade. I'm actually a fitness trainer (which means I'm actually a therapist but there's exercise involved). In all seriousness though, when I felt called to write, I felt I "should" be writing a book about fitness and nutrition since that is what I am trained in. But every time I sat down to write a book about one of those topics, I just couldn't. I was at a point in my life where everything was going wrong for me. The man I thought I was going to marry had broken up with me for the 2nd time. Due to some bad decisions and the recession of 2008, I was in an exorbitant amount of debt. I was living with a roommate that I met on Craig's List in a bad neighborhood because that's all I could afford. And I was working around the clock to try and fix it and I was exhausted. I finally just surrendered and prayed the following prayer that I heard at a Marianne Williamson lecture: "God I give my life to you. What would You have me do? I will do whatever You tell me to do, but I need You to get me out of this. Please show me the way because I am lost."

That very week, five people from different parts of my life told me that they thought I should start blogging and writing about relationships. I thought, "Can this be it? Can this be the answer I've been looking for? But disclosing the intimate details of my life would be so EMBARRASSING." I wrestled with the idea for a little while but I knew it felt right and I finally made peace with it. This is who I am. I am NOT a private person. I enjoy sharing my experiences with others, with the purpose of helping them learn and grow. The man who is going to love me one day, has to love THAT which is perhaps why the Universe has been so beneficent as to not bring him to me until I've stood up into this fully expressed version of myself. I've made a lot of mistakes in my personal relationships. Perhaps they won't have been in vain if I can help others who are a few steps behind me on the same path.

So here I am doing what God has called me to do which is write about my relationships from a spiritual perspective. And hopefully this project is going to enhance my financial status as well. I don't know what's waiting at the end of this road or what the next steps will be or how long it will take to meet "him." I can't tell you how long it will take for you to meet your "him" either. But I do know that all we have in life is the knowledge that we are living with the highest honesty and integrity with regard to ourselves. It's not an easy road to follow but it's the only way.

EPI-EPILOGUE

"The minute I heard my first love story, I started looking for you, not knowing how blind that was.

Lovers don't finally meet somewhere.

They're in each other all along." –Rumi

Oops. Maybe I spoke too soon…

As fate would have it, some time after I wrote the Epilogue for this book, I met someone. Someone amazing. And though it's relatively new, this man has no red flags that I can see. I respect and admire him. We're falling in love.

The funny thing is that he told me that I had perfect timing in connecting with him. (Who ME? The queen of awful timing with men.) But as I've said before, when someone is really for you, it is impossible to lose him. Every other man that slipped through my fingers was not for me. Or as I've once heard Marianne Williamson describe it, just as a parent will take a scissor away from a child because it could be dangerous, God will also take dangerous toys (or people) away from us.

So part of me is feeling really validated right now. Like, "Yeah I told you so. I told you gals there was a happy ending to all of this. All you have to do is stand up to do whatever it is that you feel your soul is calling you to do and he will come." But the point of this 2nd epilogue is not to gloat.

First, it's to let you know that we ALL have to swim through challenging things in life to get what we want. I've laid out my challenges in this book with the hope that some of them will resonate with you and make your learning curve a little faster.

Second, it's to demonstrate that sometimes you have to identify what you don't want to get what you do want. Every red flag in this book helped me identify the type of person I did not want. So like me, when you meet men with these flags, don't get stuck on them but rather use them to identify what you really do want. For example, if you meet a man who hides behind technology and won't make time to really connect with you, affirm that you are looking for a man that is open to deeply communicating with you on the phone and in person. If you move through life consciously, you either won't get sucked into the same red flag again, or you may get sucked in but will have the ability to remove yourself quickly. Even as I was writing this book and dating, sometimes I still found myself up shit's creek. However, this time I did indeed have a paddle.

And the final point of this epi-epilogue is to let you know that being with this man is easy, and that's truly the way it should be. When people used to tell me that a relationship should be easy I thought, "That's narcissistic! How could it be easy? I've got my issues, he's got his issues. Everyone's got their issues and it's hard to make a relationship work. Not to mention, I've done sooooo much work on myself and there's no way that any guy I'll meet will have done that much work on himself." How wrong I was.

First of all, relationships SHOULD be easy. Life is hard enough. I once heard author Caroline Myss say that whatever problems are present in a relationship, when you get married they become multiplied by ten and when you have children they become multiplied by one hundred. (Anyone who is married with kids will tell you that she's absolutely right). Petty fighting is nothing more than either partner recreating childhood dramas to get his or her emotional needs met. Yes this happens from time to time as we are not perfect, but when this sort of interaction is the rule and not the exception, you've got trouble.

Ironically, the truth of this hit me over the head the very week before I met my new love interest. I was at Planned Parenthood for my yearly well-woman check-up and there was a television screen in the waiting room flashing insights about healthy and unhealthy relationships. In my opinion, Planned Parenthood is one of the few organizations that gives due credence to the fact that being in an unhealthy relationship can ruin a woman's health. (Wonder why you got sick after that AWFUL relationship experience? Boom! This is why. As women we absolutely wilt and fall prey to disease when we remain in an unhealthy relationship and/or harbor resentment after the end of one. This has happened to me. I actually got arthritis after a particularly crushing breakup. Arthritis at the age of 32! This is no joke ladies.)

OK so back to the Planned Parenthood television screen. It read:

> **No relationship is perfect all the time. In a healthy relationship, both people feel good about the relationship most of the time. There are many things we can do to build healthy relationships. Remember that in any relationship, both people must be willing to put in the effort. One person cannot build a great relationship alone.**

It makes me really sad to say that this was a revelation for me. I always thought that the silly Planned Parenthood public service messages were for "those" people (young, uneducated, from abusive families, sex workers and drug addicts, etc.) But apparently dysfunctional relationship patterns do not discriminate because here I was, a 35-year-old, employed, financially independent, and college educated woman from a decently normal family and the fact that I am supposed to feel good about my relationship most of the time was an alien concept to me. (Like many of us, I don't remember my parents feeling particularly good about their relationship most of the time. They sucked it up and medicated or checked out in various ways to hold it together. And for the record I do not hold this against them. I'm sure I would have had a whole host of other issues if they had split. They made the best decision that they could at the time.)

And this "one person cannot build a great relationship alone, both people must be willing to put in the effort" business...Ha! I pretty much lived my entire life building relationships with men on my own. I could only laugh. Once again I was schooled (~~bitch-slapped is more accurate~~) by the simplicity of the Planned Parenthood wisdom. Are you getting the picture here? Relationships should make you feel good, happy, and loved.

On the flip side, the Planned Parenthood public service announcement had some wise yet simple words on Unhealthy Relationships:

If you feel that you're being treated badly, you probably are.

(Sadly, another major revelation for me.) This is not

rocket science here ladies. If your relationship feels good, it is. If it feels bad, get out.

OK simple wisdom aside, what about my fear that men don't work on themselves as much as women do so I'll never find someone on the same level of readiness to be emotionally available? Well admittedly my boyfriend did not do as much therapy or as many seminars as I have in my life. However, he has gone through major maturation on his own. He's one of those people that will go through something in life and *learn from it.* (Whoah! What a concept!) He is also one of those men that want nothing more than to make the woman in his life happy. These men DO exist. (I know it's hard to believe with all the nonsense that is out there nowadays but they do. Ladies, hold out for YOUR diamond in the rough.) My boyfriend IS willing to put in the effort to build a loving relationship. We came to the same place emotionally via different routes but the point is that we're here now.

We both admit that had we met earlier in life, we would not have seen each other the way we do now. We would not have been ready for each other. Our soul's evolution HAD to happen before we could be together in the way that we are now.

Is he my twin soul? I think so, but only God really knows. And the truth is, he makes me happy NOW which means that he is the perfect man for me NOW and that is all I can account for. Once again, I would like to quote the book *Twin Souls* because the following describes my experience of meeting my boyfriend in the truest way possible:

> It could almost be said that the twin appears on the scene when least needed, when each

half-soul has reached its highest point of independence in the divided state. This is also the pinnacle of aloneness. Every man and every woman must climb the mountain alone, able to stand firm against the high winds that buffet the elevated soul. It is then, out of the mist, that the twin appears, not in response to emotional need but to fulfill the deepest need of the soul. By the marvelous design of the Divine Planner, the ultimate loneliness of the spirit gives way to the first great joining and the end of loneliness forever (Joudry and Pressman 21).

When we started getting close to each other, it was so natural. I thought to myself, "Oh there you are. I've been waiting for you." Or as Rumi might have said, "You've been in me all along."

Epi - Epi - Epilogue

RESOURCES

A Course In Miracles. Mill Valley, CA: The Foundation For Inner Peace, 2007.

Allen, Patricia. *Getting To "I Do": The Secret to Doing Relationships Right!*. New York: Harper Collins, 1994.

Brene Brown, Ph.D, LMSW. *Daring Greatly: How the Courage to Be Vulnerable Transforms the Way We Live, Love, Parent and Lead*. New York: Penguin Group (USA) Inc., 2012.

Harvey, Steve. *Act Like a Lady, Think Like a Man: What Men Really Think About Love, Relationships, Intimacy, and Commitment*. New York: Harper Collins, 2009.

Joudry, Patricia, and Pressman, Maurie D. *Twin Souls: Finding Your True Spiritual Partner*. Scottsdale, Arizona: Inkwell Productions, 2009.

Pease, Allan and Barbara. *Why Men Want Sex and Women Need Love: Solving the Mystery of Attraction*. New York: Broadway Books, 2009.

Ruiz, Don Miguel. *The Four Agreements: A Practical Guide to Personal Freedom (A Toltec Wisdom Book)*. San Rafael, California: Amber-Allen Publishing, Inc., 2012.

Ryan, Christopher, and Jetha, Cacilda. *Sex at Dawn: How We Mate, Why We Stray, and What It Means for Modern Relationships*. New York: Harper Collins, 2010.

Walsch, Neale Donald. *Neale Donald Walsch on Relationships: Applications for Living*. Charlottesville, VA: Hampton Roads Publishing Company, Inc., 1999.

Williamson, Marianne. *A Return to Love: Reflections on the Principles of A Course in Miracles*. New York: Harper Collins, 1992.

Matthew Hussey's book
James Rey's book

Made in the USA
Charleston, SC
07 February 2014